C000179971

NEWCASTLE'S RAILWAYS

A VIEW FROM THE PAST

KEN GROUNDWATER

Contents

Acknowledgements

My grateful thanks to those who either proof-read, supplied pictures, provided anecdotes or simply caused me to smiasome funny occurrence or railway character that I'd long forgotten:

Ronnie Monaghan, Maurice Mowbray, Kevin Hudspith, Trevor Ermel, Alan R. Thompson, Peter J. Robinson, Ian S. Carr, David Smith, Alan Douglas, Ray Banks, Alan Jackson, 'Wally' Walton, Iain McFarlane, 'Sunderland' Dave, James Riddell, Mick Denholm, John Midcalf, Godfrey Valentine, 'Bedlington' Bob, Alan Kellas, Kester Eddy, Derek Hoogland, Dave Dinning, Derek Charlton, Dave Tyreman, Dick Taylor, Derek Knott, George and Malcolm Charlton and, of course, the Malcolm Dunnett.

Also to the most excellent and perennially cheerful 'girls' at Newcastle City Library Local Studies section, for their unstinting co-operation in picture research.

My eldest daughter Louise typed much of the manuscript — thanks Lou!

Finally, some special characters who I feel added another dimension to this story but sadly can now no longer be thanked in person: John Armstrong, John Arnott-Brown, Billy Waugh, Les Charlton and Bryce Greenfield.

Bibliography

25 Years of NER; R. Bell *(Railway Gazette)*
Coals from Newcastle; R. Finch (Terence Dalton Ltd)
The Electric Railway That Never Was; R. A. S. Hennessy (Oriel Press)
Railway Stations of the North Eastern Railway; K. Hoole (David & Charles)
Roads & Rails of Tyne & Wear (1900-1980); J. Joyce (Ian Allan)
The Wagonways of Tyneside; C. E. Lee (paper)
RCTS Locomotives class histories of the LNER Parts 1-10 ; RCTS
Past & Present No 4; Peter J. Robinson (Past & Present Publishing)
George & Robert Stephenson; L. T. C. Rolt (David & Charles)
Tomlinson's North Eastern Railway (David & Charles)
Rails between Tyne & Wear; C. R. Warn (Frank Graham Publications)
The Blyth & Tyne Branch, Parts 1-3; A. J. Wells (Northumberland County Library)
Various editions of *Trains Illustrated,* in particular May 1958 (Ian Allan)
Various editions of *Tyne & Tweed,* the Journal of the ANLHS

First published 1998

ISBN 0 7110 2616 5

Published by Ian Allan Publishing

an imprint of Ian Allan Publishing Ltd, Terminal House, Station Approach, Shepperton, Surrey TW17 8AS.

Printed by Ian Allan Printing Ltd, Riverdene Business Park, Molsey Road, Hersham, Surrey KT12 4RG.

Code 9810/B

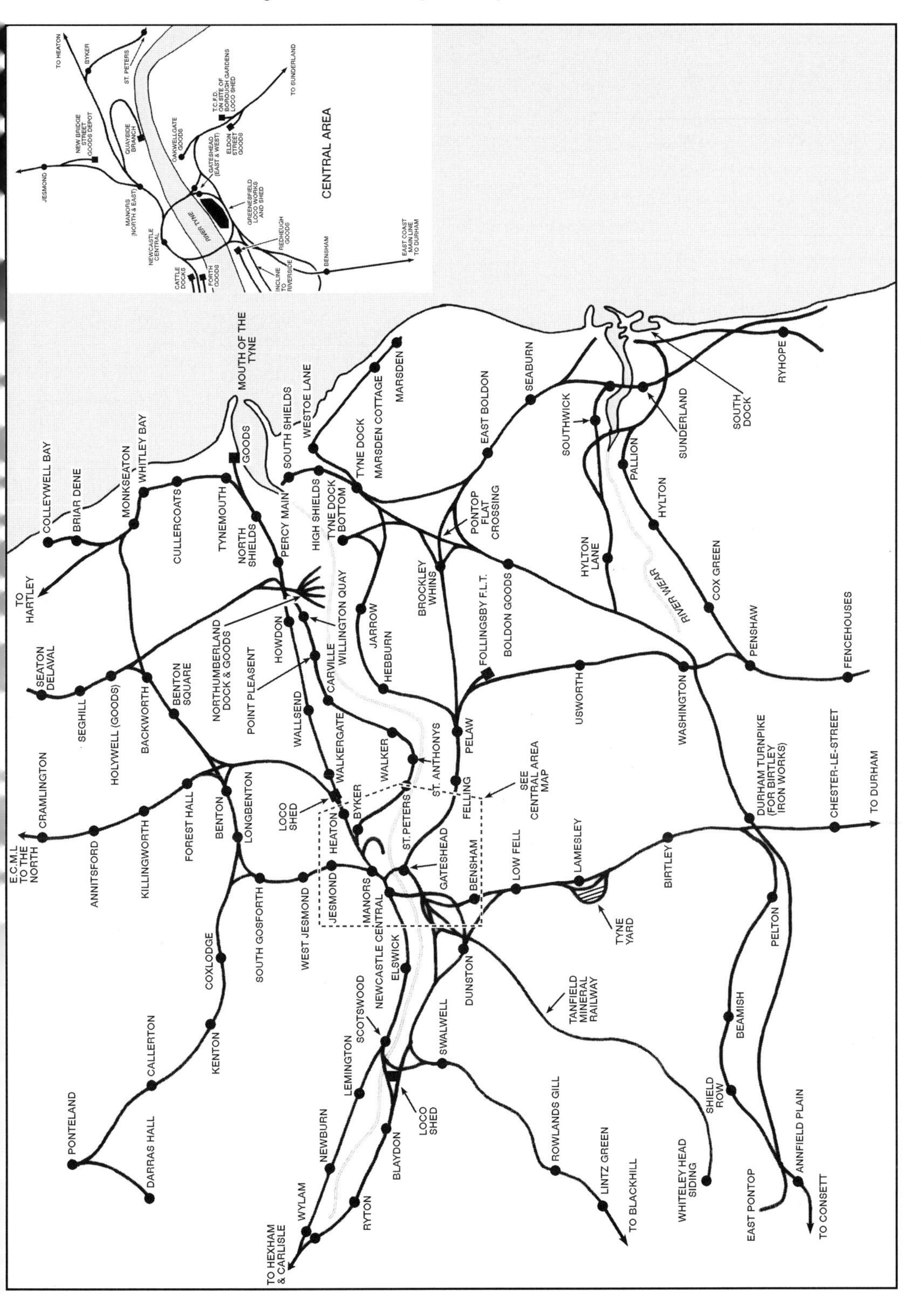
CENTRAL AREA
TO HEATON
BYKER
ST. PETERS
TO SUNDERLAND
T.C.F.D. ON SITE OF BOROUGH GARDENS LOCO SHED
NEW BRIDGE STREET GOODS DEPOT
QUAYSIDE BRANCH
OAKWELLGATE GOODS
ELDON STREET GOODS
GATESHEAD (EAST & WEST)
JESMOND
MANORS (NORTH & EAST)
GREENESFIELD LOCO WORKS AND SHED
RIVER TYNE
NEWCASTLE CENTRAL
REDHEUGH GOODS
BENSHAM
EAST COAST MAIN LINE TO DURHAM
CATTLE DOCKS
FORTH GOODS
INCLINE TO RIVERSIDE
MOUTH OF THE TYNE
COLLEYWELL BAY
BRIAR DENE
MONKSEATON
WHITLEY BAY
CULLERCOATS
TYNEMOUTH
GOODS
NORTH SHIELDS
PERCY MAIN
SOUTH SHIELDS
WESTOE LANE
HIGH SHIELDS
TYNE DOCK BOTTOM
TYNE DOCK
MARSDEN COTTAGE
MARSDEN
EAST BOLDON
SEABURN
SOUTHWICK
SUNDERLAND
SOUTH DOCK
RYHOPE
PALLION
HYLTON
HYLTON LANE
COX GREEN
RIVER WEAR
PENSHAW
FENCEHOUSES
PONTOP FLAT CROSSING
BROCKLEY WHINS
BOLDON GOODS
FOLLINGSBY F.L.T.
TO HARTLEY
SEATON DELAVAL
SEGHILL
HOLYWELL (GOODS)
BACKWORTH
BENTON SQUARE
NORTHUMBERLAND DOCK & GOODS
POINT PLEASENT
HOWDON
WILLINGTON QUAY
CARVILLE
WALLSEND
JARROW
HEBBURN
USWORTH
WASHINGTON
DURHAM TURNPIKE (FOR BIRTLEY IRON WORKS)
CHESTER-LE-STREET
TO DURHAM
CRAMLINGTON
E.C.M.L TO THE NORTH
ANNITSFORD
KILLINGWORTH
FOREST HALL
BENTON
LONGBENTON
LOCO SHED
WALKERGATE
WALKER
ST. ANTHONYS
PELAW
FELLING
SEE CENTRAL AREA MAP
HEATON
BYKER
ST. PETERS
GATESHEAD
BENSHAM
LOW FELL
LAMESLEY
BIRTLEY
TYNE YARD
PELTON
JESMOND
MANORS
NEWCASTLE CENTRAL
WEST JESMOND
SOUTH GOSFORTH
COXLODGE
KENTON
CALLERTON
PONTELAND
DARRAS HALL
ELSWICK
SCOTSWOOD
DUNSTON
TANFIELD MINERAL RAILWAY
BEAMISH
SWALWELL
LEMINGTON
LOCO SHED
ROWLANDS GILL
SHIELD ROW
ANNFIELD PLAIN
NEWBURN
BLAYDON
LINTZ GREEN
WHITELEY HEAD SIDING
EAST PONTOP
TO CONSETT
TO BLACKHILL
WYLAM
RYTON
TO HEXHAM & CARLISLE

Above: Central station in the early 1970s. A view from the west. The first three original spans of the train shed form the nucleus of this magnificent structure, thought by many to have the edge over Darlington because of the graceful curve. Between 1894 and 1895 the two additional spans to the south side were added to accommodate the growing number of platforms. The small span above old platforms 9 and 10 can be seen as curved on one side and straight on the other. This leads the eye into the fifth and straight full-size span that now also accommodates the new Regional Railways platforms that project beyond the outer wall. By the time of this view, the coast platforms at the far side (east) were de-electrified and local services supplied by DMUs. The entrance to the east platforms 1-3 was via a separate mini-concourse at the side of the Station Hotel. This area was covered with transverse roofing, seen in this view clinging to the outline of the white building — the hotel. Beyond this, at the top of the picture, is the white, triple apex-roofed parcels office that dropped conveniently to street level below for van deliveries into the city. The nearest west end platform bays were originally numbered 11-14 (and at one time 15) with their own parcels presence.
J. W. Armstrong Trust Collection

Front cover, top: Class B1 No 1100 at Newcastle Central with the 4.20pm to Carlisle, August 1947.
Colour-Rail (NE7)

Front cover, bottom left: The crossovers at the entrance to Newcastle Central station. ***Author***

Front cover, bottom right: At the head of the 2.5pm Edinburgh-Kings Cross service, No 4901 *Capercaillie* leaves Newcastle Central, 12 August 1939. ***Author***

Back cover, top: Class C3 No 5262 in Gateshead engine shed. ***W. B. Greenfield/NELPG***

Back cover, bottom: General view over the bridges, Newcastle 1959. ***E. E. Smith/Author's collection***

Below: Aerial view of Newcastle east of Central station, again in the 1970s. The large white building near the centre of the view is Swan House, the home of British Telecom on Tyneside. Immediately above is Manors station in the 'V' of the junction. The line to the left, threading under the central motorway, is the old Blyth & Tyne route to Jesmond and Benton etc. Of special interest is the route taken by imported goods from the river. This journey began from among the wharves into the Quayside Goods Yard with a push from a 'J72'. A short half-mile pull followed via a semi-circular tunnel behind an 'ESII' electric and the load was deposited at Trafalgar Yard — the limit of ECML overheads until the 1980s! Another tank engine came to do the tidying-up work and push the load around the tight curve past Argyle Street Signalbox through a tunnel and finally into the New Bridge Street Goods Depot — quite an expensive cross-town trip! New Bridge Street Goods Depot is today the site of a Warner Brothers multi-screen cinema complex. The route east of Manors is the ECML and its progress can be traced beyond to the Ouseburn viaduct into the Heaton area. The Tyne, Swing and High Level Bridges are prominent, the latter being crossed by a two-car DMU. ***University of Newcastle***

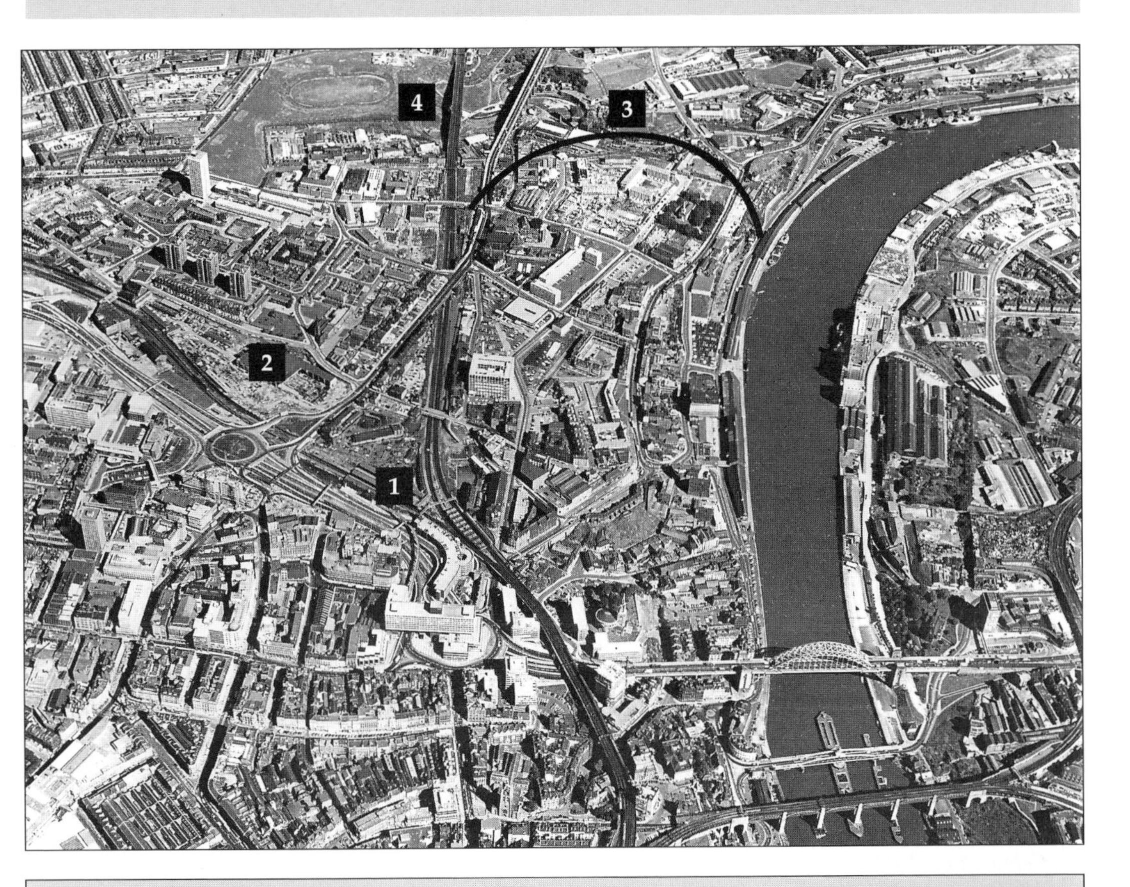

Key to aerial view

❶ Manors station

❷ New Bridge Street Goods Depot

❸ Path of Quayside branch linking Quay with Trafalgar Yard

❹ Ouseburn Viaduct

Introduction

Above: The Newcastle bank of the Tyne c1850, showing sailing craft at a quayside and a train crossing the then new High Level Bridge.
Drawing by D. Dinning

'We owe all our railways to the collieries in the north; and the difficulties which their industry overcame taught us to make railways and to make locomotives to work them...'
Part of a paper read before the Gauge Commission in 1845 by Capt J. M. Laws RN.

'The one you've got to come back for.' So runs a familiar advert for a locally brewed beverage. It could be said that few Tynesiders need any excuse to make 'the return journey'. Equally it has to be argued that Newcastle Central station is the only place to return to, in order to achieve this traditional arrival to full effect! And by arriving at Central in the heart of the city and being confronted by the three Victorian medallions above the great portico, it can be said that the return has indeed begun and the heady properties of a most atmospheric city again tasted.

The 'return' is more sought after nowadays, especially as the New York Times recently undertook a worldwide survey to establish the greatest places for atmosphere and, against hot competition, Newcastle was voted number 10 in the world — clearly the city marketing manager's dream, not only for the city but also for its railway 'arrival'.

Just what is it then that makes this 'return' so special?

It is probable that those of us who enjoy the 'return' will feel some link to many mixed ingredients. It could also be said that the effect of this particular cocktail is heightened by the larger-than-life characters whom Tyneside undoubtedly seems to spawn on a regular basis — one by-product being a rich source of raw material for local playwrights.

But do you have to be an expatriate Geordie to feel this magnetic impulse? Do you have to be in search of some spiritual northern feel-good factor? Or is it simply that we all associate times past — perhaps a childhood in the 1950s or 60s — as a period of stability in the world and in our own lives; the order of which we again search out upon making a return, to help us make sense of the infernal rush we all live through today? It is probable that those of us who enjoy the 'return' will feel some link to all the ingredients in this cocktail, one that gets well shaken from time to time and has a little bit of our own nostalgia factor added for good measure.

The journey into the city at all hours of the day and night is fortunately (for people like myself) well documented over the years and to a Geordie can be easily compared to the 'White Cliffs of Dover' syndrome, experienced on a more provincial basis. The 'return' today is not quite the industrially choking experience of yesteryear; take for instance the imagery of this piece, reported in the *Meccano Magazine* in 1934:

'The approach to the city by night (04.15 am) is weird in the extreme. Huge works are fully active and blast furnaces fill the sky with vivid glare...the station is full of activity. Huge piles of parcels traffic are being loaded into trains, shunting engines are taking a carriage off here and attaching it there...'

It also perhaps true to say that a 'return' is inextricably linked with the name of King's Cross, and this account from local journalist and writer Michael Chaplain under the heading of 'A Smile from the Gods on a Prodigal's Return' underlines the link and records the same sentiments as above, contrasting the 1980s with the new noisy 90s.

'First day of the new job and it's up and off in the dark to catch the early train north.

'As the 125 slips away from King's Cross and through the misty streets of Holloway and Finsbury Park, the window suddenly frames a view that's pure Atkinson Grimshaw, all dim shapes, gleaming lamps and scurrying figure...As I'm returning to the city where I was brought up and where I began what in pompous moments I presume to call "my career", I'm inclined to regard this as significant. An omen for the return of the prodigal...The highlight of the journey (entering Newcastle)...the jumble of towers, spires and slate roofs that fight for air on the north bank of the Tyne, looking for all the world, as another returning northerner once wrote, like a conference waiting for its picture to be taken.'

Michael goes on:

'Time was, not so very long ago, when walking out of the portico of Dobson's elegant Central, one felt oneself, by comparison with the mad maelstrom of the Euston Road, in a ghost town. Not now: the city is chock-a-block with traffic and in the (mostly) stationary taxi I ponder the causes.'

Take another 'return', observed not by a northerner but by a Hertfordshire man with a keen eye for detail and a feeling for northeastern hospitality. It is part of an account from Colin Gifford's *Steam Finale North* (Ian Allan), concerning his own special memories of late 1950s trips to this area.

'In practice I would go straight to King's Cross from work in the West End and there excitedly contemplate imminent travel [to Newcastle] within the unpretentious dignity of King's Cross. I would gravitate to No 10 platform. In the 11.50pm I had a compartment to myself and once under way could dim the lights, enabling me to see more clearly the passing scene. It was good to see dawn over Durham and then the welcoming pinheads of lights and grand silhouettes of the bridges shimmering across the River Tyne...I boarded the 06.54am Tynemouth train at Central and joined the overcoated and capped workmen on the first electric hugging the north banks of the Tyne. In privacy, at the carriage end, divided from smoky conviviality, I would slide open the door, breath deeply and listen...Byker, Walker, Point Pleasant and Percy Main were just waking shades of blue and grey contrasting with the warmth I felt for my environs and anticipation about the day ahead in the area.

'Crossing the Tyne by the fat little ferry, I was mingling with the heavy shipping and bobbing tied tugs impatient to start their day's work.

'South Shields was well awake and

Above: Perhaps not the most auspicious of birthplaces, this was nevertheless the building that housed the Board of the Stockton & Darlington Railway Co and where many of the far-reaching decisions were to be made that would eventually have such a bearing upon industrial growth in the northeast region.

The boardroom is on the first floor — and occupied the room behind the four windows in the centre above True-form shoes. ***British Railways Board/J. W. Armstrong Trust Collection***

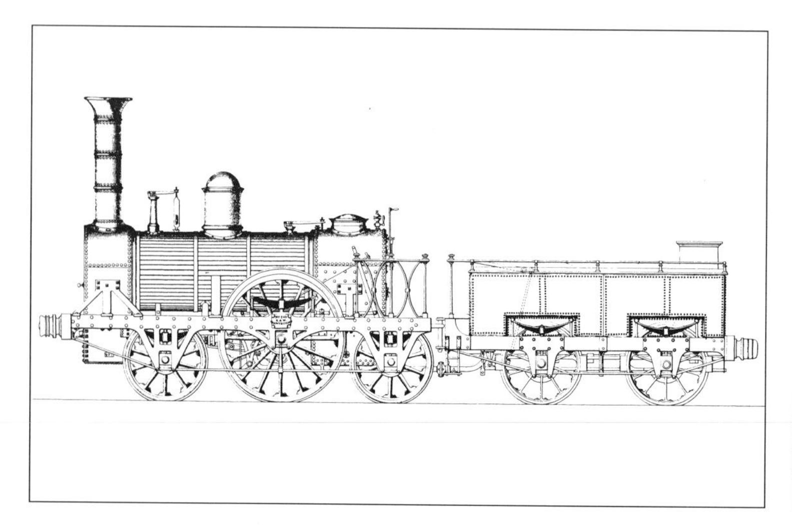

Left: R&W Hawthorn locomotive design. This is a typical design of a Newcastle engineering works in the early days of railways. This particular engine was designated an 'E' class. Numbered 245, it was destined to be one of the first engines to run in the Paris-Versailles district of France. In the same period Hawthorn also supplied similar types to the New York, Boston and Providence; Vienna and Kaab Railway; Paris-Orleans, as well as many British companies just getting off the ground. ***A. J. Wickens***

beginning to move…as I hurried past on my way to catch one of the more modern Eastleigh-built EMUs back to a fortifying breakfast in Newcastle Central — always good to arrive at — but hard to leave.'

Colin moves on to write about the great station trinity:

'The grand stations at Newcastle, Darlington and York added greatly to the strength of my attraction to the North Eastern Railway scene. Not only for the architecture but also, as they are at junctions on through routes, for their diverse and unpredictable traffic, cosmopolitan crowds and varied freight. Long may they stand!'

What follows attempts to show, through pictures, the railway metamorphoses in the Newcastle upon Tyne area and how its rich railway heritage affected the fortunes of the city and its district. From our late 20th century window we can now look back and wonder at these Victorian feats. Through imagery of the past we can reassess, as we today slide headlong into another phase of railway privatisation, just what seemed good about yesterday and, even more vital, what bouquets might be taken into the future by the new train operators to reassure us, the passengers, that over 200 years of successful and safe rail evolution here in the northeast will not go down the drain overnight.

Newcastle and Gateshead people today still continue to take great pride in the achievements of 'their' railway and the excellent systems they now enjoy by way of overhead electricity supply. It is particularly heartening to see local transport policy again being decided locally (Metro and PTE) but even more exciting for Tyneside is that the 'book of rules', as in the entrepreneurial days of Stephenson, again lies blank-paged and open on the table, waiting to be rewritten in a way that will either take Newcastle successfully into the 21st century or see a desultory list of lost opportunities result in books of this kind. Will we look back upon the late 1990s as a hiatus in the ongoing process that began on the Tyne's banks long, long ago?

Time will tell!

Below: George Stephenson's cottage at Wylam, seen in 1970, when railways still passed by the door. ***J. W. Armstrong Trust Collection***

1 Waggonways to Railways (1600 to 1850)

Above: With the low bridge (far left) as the ancient Via Media between Newcastle and Gateshead, trading was severely restricted to points below the bridge. The rights to trading on small amounts of waterfront were jealously guarded by such people as seen in this view. The steam paddle tug dates the view to about 1830 and the artist shows its presence as a matter of curiosity to himself, as it was to the onlookers of the day. The Tyne was still an unnavigable meandering stream to all intents and purposes and this, plus resistance, to change helped repulse competition, a situation that satisfied the city fathers maintaining their superiority along much of the waterfront to the river mouth. Coal was to act as the catalyst for change. Coal export was then a seriously slow business on Tyneside. It involved many manual transhipments and the London market was not satisfied. The presence of this steam tug was a veiled threat not only to the owners but to the keelmen themselves. Steam was not going to go away. The positive changes that followed with the creation of the Tyne Improvement Commission eventually saved this lucrative London market.
Courtesy of Northern Rock Building Society

The discovery and mining of the Great Northern Coalfield opened up an area consisting of hamlets and small towns lining the banks of a still rural and shallow River Tyne. This development began in the 16th century and by the 18th century Newcastle was a large black dot on the industrial map of the world, and described by a contemporary as:

'Everywhere... industry, resource, and expansion, coal staith, chemical works, forges, electrical lighting laboratories, warehouses,

merchants' offices, steamships, railway trains, without end, without number — from Shields to Scotswood there is not its like in any 13-mile of river the world over.'
R. W. Johnson; The Making of the Tyne; 1895

If a single person can be said to have acted as the catalyst for rail development in the region, then most would nominate William Beaumont of Nottingham. In 1604 Beaumont brought then-advanced thinking from his home area to a Tyneside eagerly anticipating this next phase. He assisted financially in the building of a 'waggonway' and though built of wood, it was nevertheless generally accepted as being the first reliable 'way' for horsedrawn carts to pass on. It was needed, for as the easily worked coal measures were receding from the river, the searching tentacles had to move ever further inland and the logistics of transport were becoming impossible as the mileages between collieries and the waiting boats increased. The rails gave the Northumbrians the means to overcome the problem.

The next important development seems to have been William Chapman's experiments at Heaton, in cast-iron 'way' with a rack or toothed notches to counteract slippage on gradients. By 1797 the Lawson Main Colliery line to the Tyne was iron, and developments moved quickly from this point. Through the early 19th century the iron-railed waggonways that followed began to cover the landscape of Northumbria — so much so that the many black tentacles across the still verdant landscape appalled environmentally-conscious landowners (though they quickly changed their tune upon news of the land-rent or wayleave they would be getting!).

While all this was going on, Trevithick, Blackett, Blenkinsop, Hedley, Hackworth and finally Stephenson brought the steam locomotive to a degree of reliability that instantly placed Tyneside and particularly Newcastle into the forefront of world technology. The age of steam annexed onto the latter stages of the relentlessly advancing industrial revolution was to power up the Victorian era into a frenzy of railway building and set fire to the rest of the world. Newcastle as the nuclear point!

As scientific and historical textbooks tell us, important discoveries need 'the correct conditions prevailing'. Newcastle's good luck was to be in the right place at the right moment with the available resources, and the 'accident of time' which so favoured it was the ease of coal-pickings alongside the Tyne and the sudden insatiable demand for the black stuff in London. Once the coal trade was established with London agents and Newcastle had beaten off the only other active threats (from South Wales and the Lothians of Scotland), the City Fathers took full advantage of their favoured position and began to so satisfy London that they monopolised the market. London had no choice and paid up, and eventually some of this money found its way back into funding the waggonway development that was to lead to the introduction of steam.

The resultant transport revolution was not just limited to railways. Steam was universal to all forms of manufacturing and next to take advantage of this accident in resources was the Tyne itself. The Stephenson engineering empire based in South Street, Newcastle, was to link with men of even greater vision in wider fields; Hawthorn, Leslie, Palmer and Armstrong were just some of the men who were to transform the banks of the Tyne into the sort of 'industrial hell' often portrayed to good effect by the contemporary painter Maddox-Brown.

Newcastle was by now, the mid-19th century, not only the hub of the London coal trade, but the world centre for the construction of iron-clad fighting ships. Yet strangely, and almost imperceptibly, the fickle world of business resulted in Tyneside losing its hold upon the very industry that underpinned all this expansion — railway construction and engineering. In fact the very industry for which a gambling man of the time would have wagered Newcastle to be forever remembered. The ideal conditions, as discussed earlier, now favoured York and Darlington, which, with George Hudson thereabouts, were quick to take on the railway engineering mantle of the north. (A sad addendum to this story is the 1995 closure of the ABB railway workshops in York, which ended continuous railway production of some kind in this area going back to 1813.)

The new 'iron age' failed to propel Newcastle's railway entrepreneurs into a further chapter for many complex reasons, but undoubtedly the logistics involving Teesside, (easy access to ironstone) and the increasingly cramped Tyneside river-banks had some bearing on this drift to Teesside.

This then was the start of it all, not just for Newcastle folk, but for travel throughout the world, which would never be quite the same again.

2
NER Growth (1850-1930)

By the 1860s the railway companies had become great powers in the land. Nobody's life was unaffected by them, even if only in a small way. In the northeast, the North Eastern Railway was growing, by amalgamations, by takeovers and by building new routes on its own account. By 1874 it was substantially complete and by then included the Stockton & Darlington and the stubborn Blyth & Tyne in its list of constituents; the latter had held out for years. It now managed some 1,300 miles of route and several hundred stations, of which Newcastle Central was the busiest.

The years from 1854 to 1866 are regarded by historians as seeing the last and greatest fling of station construction in Britain, but, like many great stations, Newcastle Central did not then take on its greatest form — not yet. Further developments were to come as the century progressed. Meanwhile the North Eastern Railway was busily securing itself.

From 1874 the NER concentrated on consolidating its gains and began 'laying out its stall' to capitalise on its strong position, as it moved into a period when its bank balance was healthy. Captains of industry were wooed onto Board positions and moving forward with big business became very much the hallmark of the NER by the turn of the century.

It is said that the peak was reached in 1914. Scanning through the trade journals of the time, it is indisputable that the NER was an influential concern, and there was a real company pride in being an NER employee, which showed in the attitude of the staff, from the top officers to the youngest recruit. Unfortunately for the NER, this success also focused outside attention upon those managing that success; head-hunting by other organisations, from powerful companies to Government departments, began on such a scale that had not World War 1 intervened, the NER may have been seriously depleted of its top brass.

Left: An Atlantic creeps cautiously over the High Level Bridge and into Newcastle in this historic view from c1920. Few photographers caught these last moments of the empty and condemned village of Pipewellgate — this tightly packed community had been ravaged by cholera 70 years previous and was not to survive much longer. Behind the camera are the foundations and high walls that held up Greenesfield Works and loco sheds. On the Newcastle side the 1920s skyline shows the old keep, (one of the taller buildings) adjacent to the station. ***J. W. Armstrong Trust Collection***

Right: Neville Street and Central station soon after construction (c1860). The desolation speaks volumes compared with the noisy times to come. Still to be built was the extension that became the hotel wing of the station. The east end entrance and the electric lighting are also missing. The building to become known as the Victoria and Comet Hotel is already standing opposite the station. Beyond, the row of houses seen crossing the distant landscape was soon to be erased from the map for road widening. The view of the station roof was to last but a short time. ***Courtesy Newcastle City Library***

At its zenith the NER could cope with anything. It had the 'blue riband' for speed over the York-Darlington racetrack section. It boasted elegance of conveyance second to none with its well appointed East Coast stock, and was able, by the sheer brute force of its plucky mineral engines, to move mountains of coal and steel — and did on a daily basis. This efficiency of movement was only really touched again in the 1960s with the advent of merry-go-round freight trains and High Speed passenger trains.

It is strange to relate however that the 1870s were the financial peak of the company in terms of profitability returning to shareholders. Thereafter, and in spite of continued success, the expansion was tempered by rising costs, led by factors such as worker-power and 'operational difficulties'. The system had reached a watershed — the sort of financial crossroads that would today see a takeover and subsequent 'paring-down' back to profitability.

In the 1870-75 period over 50% of coal moved by the NER was 'landsale' (coal intended for internal consumption, such as ironworks, manufacturing industries and household use). With the continuing industrialisation of the more advanced parts of the world, the international demand for northeast coal soared and by 1875 exporting had become the most important part of the coal business. Staithes sprung up at every river promontory between the Coquet and the Tees. But however great the scale of this activity became, the NER did not forget its less profitable passenger business. Among other ventures, by 1894 the enlargement of Newcastle Central was complete.

In 1904 through running to Middlesbrough commenced with the completion of the Durham Coast route and consequently Central became even busier. The company now controlled 1,670 route miles and to cap this, at what might today be termed the NER's second 'happy-time', the company announced that a splendid new headquarters was to be constructed at York — still then regarded by many as historically England's second city.

International tensions were growing in Europe and the imminence of World War 1 deflated these constructional energies; instead resources were moved to the construction of siding and storage space that it was anticipated would be needed for the coming war effort. Whatever it meant, one thing was evident: the NER was now in retreat.

Summing up this period of growth and expansion, it is an undisputed fact that the key event which was to change the company's fortunes for ever was the appointment of George Gibb as Chairman. His fresh and radical approach not only pushed the NER to the forefront of British railway companies but made 'NER good practice' an example to be followed by many successful English businesses thereafter. His methods were subsequently adopted by the LNER as the best practices available, and his reorganisation of the Traffic Department was to last through to 1975 in many railway offices; only then did the TOPS computer-based accountancy systems finally replace methods introduced in the 19th century.

This great expansionist era led to another milestone in the years approaching 1914, when George Hudson's dream of the NER becoming the country's greatest dock-owning organisation became reality.

All this progress focused on the company's operational dexterity in keeping the traffic moving. A major advance in Newcastle Central's ability to cope, at one of the vital junctions in the whole system, came about in 1912, when the great diamond crossing at the east end of the layout was relaid in cast manganese steel. This new material would give 12 years' life to trackwork in a key location that had been a constant source of anxiety to the NER Permanent Way Department. The huge cast block was dropped into position on a rainy Saturday/Sunday slack period and was described by a contemporary engineer as the most complicated rail intersection then in use. The diamond had to cope with over 1,000 train movements daily at this time.

Other developments were helping operational efficiency. In 1854 Newcastle Central was still signalled with the old low disc or square types of signal but these were steadily replaced by the more familiar semaphores, survivors of which are still to be seen today along the Newcastle & Carlisle line. The NER's first electro-pneumatic signalling was installed at Tyne Dock in 1905 and it was not long before this new technology was being introduced at Newcastle Central. Meanwhile, in 1903-4 the suburban lines between Newcastle and the coast were equipped for third-rail electrification, another technological innovation for its time.

However, things were not running so smoothly on the staff relations front and it was not until 1911 that relationships between

Below: Benton, on the northern leg of the coast circle, was at the apex of two north-south junctions that connected with the ECML. It is noticeable that at the time of this 1906 picture the north spur wasn't commissioned although the signalling was in place. A brand new NER electric has stopped at the diamond 'stop' sign. Nearby an advert speaks of Murtons waterproof clothing — perhaps a forerunner of locally made Barbour clothing? Today's many Benton commuters benefit from the latest form of electric power in the shape of the overhead supply to MetCam Metro trams. ***Newcastle City Library***

Above: NER No 516, Darlington works-built in 1883, is a relatively modern machine at the time of this picture of 'the ramp' opposite Gateshead Greenesfield shed, c1890. It stands across from the Brandling extension lines separating this raised standage area from the main shed at Gateshead. It was locally known as 'the ramp' due to the steeply graded access up from the Newcastle & Carlisle shed at Chaytors Bank. The windows of Askew Road 'Tyneside flats' prior to demolition in the 1920s provided an excellent viewing gallery although the constant black pall of smoke emanating from Greenesfield did nothing to enamour the railway to those responsible for the contents of clothes lines on washday. ***J. W. Armstrong Trust Collection***

Above: Percy Main was the scrapyard for countless engines prior to the establishment of Darlington works in the early 20th century as the central scrapping point for the NER. Amidst the scrap is R. W. Hawthorn-built No 1495, dating from 1894 to a design by McDonald. Many locomotives of this period had short lives as development was proceeding rapidly, the successful NER 'R' class (later 'D20') made their appearance in 1899 making many earlier locomotives obsolete at a stroke. ***J. W. Armstrong Trust Collection***

Above: A raised standage area was provided opposite 'the ramp' adjacent to the main shed area at Greenesfield, Gateshead. As evolution rapidly altered the requirements of the depot this area was subsequently levelled to incorporate the space adjacent to the Pacific shed, near the end of the King Edward VII Bridge. This levelling allowed light engines to move more easily in and out, via the bridge. In this view of c1890, 1883 Darlington-built No 620 stands outside the shed and displays its ownership via the brass splasher plate.
J. W. Armstrong Trust Collection

management and staff settled down after a long period of turbulence, when national standards of wages and conditions were finally adopted as the basis for future negotiations. This process had begun in 1890, when Henry Tennant made railway history by agreeing to meet a trade union official to talk about grievances; the first move in British railway history towards official recognition of a union. It was to upset the Government and other railway company managements but it was a step that showed the willingness of the NER to move forward with a resolve to keep the traffic moving.

Another innovation came in 1909 with the introduction of mineral loading bonuses to crews who achieved more than the standard shift tonnage. These again continued in some form through to the decline in mineral traffic in the 1980s, which is perhaps an indication of how much more difficult these agreements are to remove than they are to set up in the first place!

The 1920s showed a steady mean of achievement on the NER performance graph but with falling profits as labour became more and more expensive. Shareholders became nervous. The Grouping of railway companies into the Big Four in 1923 did some good in steadying nerves but the Great War had damaged business to some countries beyond repair. Export figures from Dunston and Tyne Dock in these years were never to equal those of the first decade of the century.

What could the LNER now do to reverse the slide?

Above: Fifteen years after our earlier view of the main portico entrance (page 13), and from the other side, it can be seen that the age of the electric tram (albeit single-deckers) has arrived with vengeance. Coachmen from the horse-drawn carriages laze in the late afternoon sun, perhaps reconsidering their profession in light of this new threat. In another 10 years (1915) horses would be predominantly employed in the carriage of goods with the advent of the motor bus threatening the tram in the next stage of the evolution of passenger transportation outside of the station. ***Newcastle City Library***

Right: Newcastle Central portico c1885. Dobson's fine work is seen here as it was intended — uncluttered. This was a time when there was room for two horse carriages to pass at the entrance. The scene is little altered today: St John's Church stands alongside Bewick Street, the County Hotel may have expanded a little but Lockhart's cocoa rooms grew into the Victoria & Comet Hotel, now an Irish 'theme' pub. The big clock continues to tell Geordies how long they have before their train time. ***Newcastle City Library***

Left: A floral extravaganza accosted the passenger of 1910 when entering the general room at Heddon-on-the-Wall. This was most probably a candidate for the NER's best-kept general room competition, part of the greater competition of best-kept station, and is certainly making best use of the heat from the stove which is lost somewhere within the foliage. A look at the NER's official passenger bookings for the year of 1911, shows an increase in 23 passengers over the previous year. One hopes these extra travellers had no problem with pollen! ***Newcastle City Library***

Left: To the east of Heddon was Newburn station; this 1910 view shows the still-pristine structure. Tyneside was thriving at this time and employment in this particular area was now buoyant with the factories of Elswick just down the road. The population here had risen by 1,000 from 1900 and bookings from Newburn reached a high of 106,798 in the next year (although the townships of Throckley and Walbottle contributed to this figure). ***Newcastle City Library***

Left: A grim reminder that the evolution towards the excellent safety record of today's railways was not without its difficulties in the early years. We may take for granted such things as electrical interlocking and track circuit control but enginemen in the 19th century worked long hours in extreme conditions, and high casualty figures often resulted. William Stephenson was such an individual. His gravestone at Tweedmouth includes the statement that: '...he opened the Newcastle & Berwick Railway in July 1847 by taking the first train of passengers from Tweedmouth to Newcastle'.
Berwick Advertiser

Above: A Gateshead Works engine brought fresh from the paint shop to the expanse of Tyne Dock to be photographed in the spring of 1906. Classed as a '4CC' by the NER and as a 'C8' by the LNER, only two of these compound Atlantics were built, the product of the very gifted Chief Draughtsman at Gateshead, Walter Smith. Smith got a generous budget for these designs and they proved excellent value for money at £4,661 each. No 730 was based at Gateshead shed for much of its career, being withdrawn in 1934 having run 752,939 miles. Its proudest moment was hauling Queen Alexandra from Edinburgh to York in 1906, for the first time without a change of loco at Newcastle. The King Edward Bridge had just been opened. With the arrival of Gresley Pacifics in 1924, No 730 was relieved of top link duties. When further Pacifics arrived at Gateshead in 1930, it was seldom used and ended its days at the back of the shed at Heaton in January 1935.
British Railways Board

Right: The construction team for the 'A1' Pacific order at Darlington Works pose with the first to be outshopped: No 60130 *Kestrel*, on 28 September 1948.
BR/J. W. Armstrong Trust Collection

Above: Although the proverbial dark-clouds of war were not yet visible, they were but four months away when Heaton's shedded *Bittern* brought the 10.5am from London under the various bridges to the north of Lamesley towards Newcastle. This service followed 5min behind the 'Flying Scotsman' and was known amongst railwaymen as the '*Junior* Scotsman'. The delightfully landscaped 'permanent way' was a feature of prewar travel that, sadly, has never been rediscovered since. It is perhaps worth mentioning here that these features were an inherent part of the 'Silver Jubilee' package created in the mid-1930s to give the passenger the most pleasant 'total' experience. ***W. B. Greensfield/NELPG***

Left: An afternoon view of the Neville Street approach to Central, c1910. Trams, horsedrawn carriages and bicycles dodge around pedestrians who still walk wherever they desire in an area where this would now be suicidal. Forth Banks Lane is signed on the right on the building which today fills the role of the InterCity Telesales Centre crèche. ***Courtesy Newcastle City Library***

Left: One of the earliest known surviving photographs of inside the station, shortly after its completion. The original low platform height is unmistakable. Virtually no integrated buildings are seen other than the main block. It is apparent that the bay in the foreground is only a few yards away from being able to join up with the west end bays, and the coaches in the background stand where the new travel centre now is. ***Courtesy Newcastle City Library***

Left: The view from Pilgrim Street Signalbox towards Central station, at the location now described as Dean Street crossover. An indication of the swathe of old (and in this case cholera-ridden) property in Castle Garth that was cleared by the building of the East Coast route is shown by some of the remaining pantiled roofs seen at line level (but also soon to go). The city at this point is high above river level, the railway arriving from the North on viaducts and arches, c1920. ***J. W. Armstrong Trust Collection***

Left: This view must be approximately 1910 as both gas and electric lighting are on display (was this a publicity picture for the new electric?). A fine double 'goldfish bowl' lamp holder stands on a plinth. It is long since removed; however, a similar design was due to reappear in changes planned for 1997. The water fountain is close by, slatted seating is sprinkled throughout and a fascinating collection of dispensing machines adorns the area between Platforms 4 and 5. ***Courtesy Newcastle City Library***

Centre left: Meeting under the clock was always easy when it happened to be this large Potts of Leeds clock. Much trivia betrays the fashions of the time, with wicker baskets strewn about here and there. Engine No 1860 stands on a set of vehicles and awaits the road. The early 'glasshouse' signalbox has good views over the northbound bays and on the far right can be seen the dim silhouette of the old engine *Billy* upon its plinth.
Courtesy Newcastle City Library

Below left: Stephenson locomotive *Billy* on display between platforms 9 and 10. The plaque on the plinth records that it was presented to the Mayor and Corporation of Newcastle on 9 June 1881, the centenary of Stephenson's birth. *Billy* was removed some years later to a plinth at the Newcastle end of the High Level Bridge adjacent to the famous Bridge Hotel (where many NELPG schemes have been hatched). It seems to have been removed to the Science Museum in Newcastle's Exhibition Park in the 1940s and can be seen today at Middle Engine Lane, near Percy Main. ***J. W. Armstrong Trust Collection***

Left: This view, believed taken about 1903, shows *Billy* in position at the end of the High Level Bridge. ***J. W. Armstrong Trust Collection***

Centre left: Manors (Pilgrim Street) Signalbox interior with frame and peripheral kit in the 1930s. The diagram as viewed shows to the left the route towards Newcastle and to the lower right the four-track main line to Edinburgh. The upper right route is to Benton. The box was manned by one signalman with a booking lad, and bearing in mind the density of traffic here, it must have seen the two working flat out for much of the time. The box had disappeared by the end of the 1940s, its work transferred to the newer Manors Station Box. ***J. W. Armstrong Trust Collection***

Left: 'J' class 4-2-2 No 1521, a typical 1889 product of Thomas W. Worsdell, depicted here on a fairly typical postcard of the 1920-30 era (in this case credited to G. Smith of North London). The 'Js' had a relatively short life as shown, as technology rapidly advanced and they were subsequently rebuilt by Wilson Worsdell in 1895. They were numbered 1517-26. No 1521 had the honour of representing the NER at the Edinburgh Exhibition of 1890. ***J. W. Armstrong Trust Collection***

Left: Only a few years after the 1906 opening of the King Edward Bridge, Class Z No 735, itself only months out of works, makes its way south off the bridge with an express passenger working. The 'Zs' were some of the first engines to be built outside the NER following the 1910 decision to cease building at Gateshead, No 735 being constructed by North British at Hyde Park Works, Glasgow. It is said the class proved popular with enginemen, which is borne out by their use as standby cover for the 'Flying Scotsman' right up to World War 2. It is interesting to note, and the RCTS histories confirm this, that these 'Z' engines exchanged tenders with the then newly built 'Q6' locomotives as an improvement. Ironically some 'Z' tenders were returned to 'Q6s' when withdrawals began in 1943, and one in particular saw service with No 63346 right up to the end of steam in the northeast in 1967 — a tender story!
R. J. Purves/T. J. Ermel Collection

Centre left: This 4-4-0 wheel arrangement with double splasher was a trademark of NER loco designers from the 1890s and was a style that dominated passenger working in the area until the late 1920s. This class came to be Class D22 after the LNER was formed in 1923. No 1540 ran from 1890 until 1929; No 1537 was the last in service and was withdrawn in 1935. By that time the Gresley Pacifics dominated main-line passenger work through Newcastle.
J. W. Armstrong Trust Collection

Below left: The roof of Fitzgerald's Bridge Hotel continues to be a landmark today at the Newcastle end of the High Level Bridge. An NER electric set crosses the Tyne into the 'grand junction' area below the old keep viewing point. Arriving from South Shields, it is passing a Class J39. Brett's oil and grease works still thrives today and has extended into the Jubilee Wharf site, once belonging to Gateshead Corporation.
A. R. Thompson Collection

Left: The emergence of electric trams and eventually motorbuses caused a major slippage in NER finances in the early 20th century. One economy idea tried was steam railcars, and *Phoenix* (they took their names mainly from stagecoaches) ran from 1928 until 1946. She was a two-cylinder model and worked mostly on Tyneside during her career, although her final days were in the Hull area. In the 1930s/40s they could be seen on branch lines all over the LNER. Their natural successors are the single car Class 153s now evident in this area and also attempting to steady the slide to road traffic.
J. W. Armstrong Trust Collection

Left: The Tyne's banks in 1887, from a point just below Gateshead Greensfield Shed and Works, and known as the 'Rabbit Banks'. There is much of interest in this view. Dominating the skyline is the cathedral, the castle keep and, on the High Level Bridge, a gantry-mounted signalbox which looks a most precarious posting for any signalman (especially one with sleepwalking tendencies!). The huddle of buildings on the Newcastle side are where a hotel and offices stand today, with promenade walks that would astound the industrialists of old. ***Courtesy Gateshead Central Library***

Right: Another view of the 'C7' class; No 2210 was one of the Darlington-built batch in 1920. It is said they were always referred to by railwaymen as 'Zs' — their old classification. They were found to be 'acceptable' on the flat NER stretches but poor hill climbers on the route north. They were superseded on main line duties in the Newcastle area first by the Raven Pacifics in 1923, then by the Gresley Pacifics a few years later.
J. W. Armstrong Trust Collection

Right: One of perhaps hundreds of similar but different views taken over the years from this location — the castle keep — down onto the great crossing. This postcard view of about 1905 makes the accustomed boast of 'The largest railway crossing in the World' and so we were brought up to believe! This is one area of the station where a complete record of even the smallest change is recorded on an almost weekly basis! At this time the canopies extended well beyond the main train shed roof but the large No 1 Signalbox had not yet been incorporated into the north end gantry. ***J. W. Armstrong Trust Collection***

Left: Manors (ECML) platforms c1915 show a very well ordered and tidy affair. The neat flowerbeds and litter-free running area contrast with the jumble of power lines that clutter the air space. As the empty platforms hint, the railway is fighting a long battle against bus and tram, not wholly successfully in spite of the recent electrified option for the suburban lines users. ***Beamish Museum***

Below left: By 1935 quite a lot has changed at the city eastern approach. A new crossover has gone in between the up and down main, the gantry has been resited to include the New Bridge Street curve from Trafalgar Yard sidings and is controlled from Argyle Street Signalbox. The LNER has removed the flowerbeds but functional necessity dictates that spent ballast shares passenger facilities. The LNER modern image lamps look on as 'A3' No 2744 brings the up 'Flying Scotsman' through, watched by a solitary figure. ***W. B. Greenfield /NELPG***

Right: Track gangs at work, Pilgrim Street Signalbox. With Manors station in the background and Manors (Pilgrim Street) Signalbox above, a combination of Newcastle and Manors length gangs are engaged in radical alteration work early one Sunday morning c1910. It is interesting to note that what today would be young men's work is here showing an age profile of approximately 40. Flat caps were de rigueur and the bowler-hatted foreman clearly stands out. Collars and ties are common and spirits are good — this is an overtime job! ***J. W. Armstrong Trust Collection***

Above: Re-laying the crossing. With help from two Thomas Smith cranes, two and a half days were devoted to the once-frequent replacement of the diamond crossing trackwork. Manganese steel slowed down the wear rate, thereby reducing the frequency and saving considerable costs, not to mention disruption to services. It can be seen that the High Level Bridge routes are all stopped, with all trains using the King Edward Bridge, and a flagman protects workers from the remaining through line. The crossing reached its height of complexity between 1895 and 1904, when even bay Platforms 1 and 2 had a route over the High Level Bridge. ***J. W. Armstrong Trust Collection***

Above: No 3 Signalbox, before and after. These pictures of Newcastle No 3 in the 'V' of the main line south and the west line route, show its commanding position but were meant as an official 'past and present record' of cosmetic improvements. The Civil Engineer was concerned that the collection of small huts gave a run-down impression to travellers and ordered this area be cleaned up! It would be interesting to have answers to some questions, such as: How long did the wallflowers survive this claustrophobic nightmare? Was this the NER's smallest garden? Was a full time gardener employed for this important display? Was it watered from the signalbox above?
Both E. Brack Collection

3
LNER Days (1931-1948)

Though the NER became a part of the new London & North Eastern Railway at the 1923 Grouping, it took several years for the new organisation to fully assert itself over the old order. It seems fairer to take the years of centralised LNER control as really beginning with the 1930s.

This period began full of hope. The long, slow recovery from postwar industrial blight seemed to be well under way but then new build orders on the Tyne began slowing in a dramatic fashion. The world was experiencing a bankruptcy hiatus, but for the LNER, although it was not to know it then, the 1930s were to be the final glorious heyday for steam as the supreme prime mover on the main-line railway in this country.

In seeking an image of this era, we are particularly fortunate to have the co-operation of the North Eastern Locomotive Preservation Group in making available photographs taken by Major Bryce Greenfield. Bryce was photographing diligently throughout this golden age and even into the war years. He perhaps more than anyone captured the excitement of these times by enthusiastically logging the passing scene alongside the East Coast main line in the Gateshead / Newcastle area as early trials of sometimes semi-finished engines raised the pulse of bystanders and an inkling of what lay ahead gradually grew into reality.

Fortunately, Bryce photographed everything that was passing in those days and gave us an excellent 'snapshot' record of this brief but heady era.

Away from the main line, the goods activity of the area may have been less well documented but the northeast's economic difficulties as a whole, a reflection of the

Above: The huge Parsons plant on the Coast Road forms a backcloth to this portrait of a Gresley racehorse — No 2581 *Neil Gow* — turning on the 70ft turntable at Heaton shed, 2 May 1937. ***W. B. Greenfield/NELPG***

Above: Giving a full flavour to the station ambiance at Newcastle in 1936, engine No 2575 (later to be 60076) *Galopin* stands in sunny splendour at the head of a Scottish express. Alongside is a wooden-bodied NER EMU, dating from 1904, awaiting departure 'all stations' to the coast. ***W. B. Greenfield/NELPG***

Below: With the streamlined Pacifics in general circulation by 1937 it meant that the older Class A1s, originally diagrammed to work the crack east coast expresses, were 'cascaded' to lesser links. One frequent pairing until 1937 was No 4472 *Flying Scotsman* with the train of the same name. Here we see it hurrying the crack express south from Newcastle at Chester-le-Street in 1 August 1936. Today, No 4472 is the only surviving example of the unstreamlined Gresley Pacifics. It was purchased upon withdrawal in January 1963 by Mr Alan Peglar and is now owned by Dr Tony Marchington. ***W. B. Greenfield/NELPG***

Right: With the breach in the station wall leading through to the station hotel (and Neville Street) behind, Class A1 No 2563 *William Whitelaw* reposes in Platform 8 and awaits time at the head of a down train.

Built by North British, Glasgow, in 1924 it was renamed *Tagalie* in July 1941, being withdrawn from service in 1964 after 40 years service. ***W. B. Greenfield/ NELPG***

worldwide problems, were extremely well covered. Such events as the Jarrow March, a parade of 207 unemployed workmen from Jarrow to London in October 1936, at the depths of the depression, are now part of British history. To the LNER, looking to the 'small profit' passenger as its likely financial saviour, an end to the recession and regrowth of employment in the industrial regions was an essential first step to prosperity.

How odd it is therefore to reflect back on this time of contradiction. On the one hand, the LNER was finding the money and resources to build sets of lavishly appointed, silver rexine-finished coaches and a new fleet of 35 expensive, streamlined locomotives, while on Tyneside the staiths lay idle, staff in goods yards were laid off and ships everywhere skulked against buoys, laid up in forgotten estuarys. All around the goods departments a massive mothballing exercise had been going on for almost three years but a slow recovery from 1937 came conveniently just in time for the build up towards another world war.

It is today a matter only for conjecture to imagine the public reaction if the 'Silver Jubilee' had flopped. The train was not just a commercial but a political exercise and perhaps in those now far-off 1930s brought a welcome chink of light (and hope) through the darkness of depression, saying to the people, 'the worst is over — look to the future!'

So it was then in 1935 that not only Bryce Greenfield and his chums eagerly awaited the sight of streamliners at Newcastle Central. The station was filled with unemployed people eager to get a view into this new future and simply say that they had seen the 'Silver Jubilee'. Factories on Tyneside applied to the LNER for permission to use the streamlined logo on their products. Toffees bought in corner shops displayed the silver shape; everyone on Tyneside was keen to associate with this new image of success. In perhaps one of the first national displays of media hype, the LNER indulged itself in a hundred new posters by successful artists of the day and for three years Newcastle Central was a magnet not just to small boys but also their mams and dads, grannies and grandas. The LNER had pulled off one of the first multimedia coups in the western world.

Cruelly, World War 2 wrecked the LNER's infrastructure, so much so that it was to be well

into the 1950s before the railway in these parts crept out from under the grey war shroud. A 'fire-fighting' management style through the war years and the austerity that followed diverted attention from all that was good and had been achieved in the glorious time from 1935 to 1939. On the East Coast it could be said that it was in 1953 and the first full year of the new 'Elizabethan' express that the positives finally began to tip over the negativeness of recovery mode.

By now, of course, the world had moved on, the car was firmly established and increasing in number by almost a quarter of a million machines a year. The railways of Britain needed a new direction.

Above: The early days of streamlined operations in the area saw test runs to 'prove' the practicability of point-to-point timings, not only for the London-Newcastle route but also to Edinburgh. Bryce Greenfield caught this historic view on a dank 26 September day in 1936 when the third of Gresley's streamlined Pacifics — *Silver King* — sets the pace with the 'Silver Jubilee' set and the recording vehicle on a high-speed test run to Edinburgh. It has just passed the site of the Wills (tobacco) factory and is about to pass Little Benton farm at a speed already in excess of 60mph. ***W. B. Greenfield/NELPG***

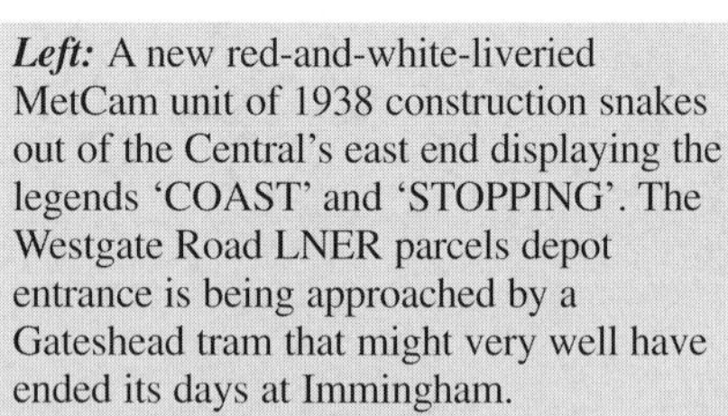

Left: A new red-and-white-liveried MetCam unit of 1938 construction snakes out of the Central's east end displaying the legends 'COAST' and 'STOPPING'. The Westgate Road LNER parcels depot entrance is being approached by a Gateshead tram that might very well have ended its days at Immingham.
A. R. Thompson Collection

Left: The steam-intensive days of the late 1930s boom on the railway in this region saw both Heaton and Gateshead sheds' resources stretched to the limit. It took only a minor hiccup in the servicing cycle at a depot for a major log-jam to develop. At Heaton, just such a thing occurred on 29 May 1937 when Class A1 Pacific No 2582 *Sir Hugo* (later 60083) joins the procession of engines awaiting attention.
W. B. Greenfield/NELPG

Left: A view from Pilgrim Street signalbox over the considerable acreage that made up Manors North and East stations. Locomotive-hauled NER vehicles are overtaken by another NER MetCam electric unit coming off the Jesmond arm of the coastal circle. There is much interesting detail here: down below, on the corner, is the original HQ of the Tyne & Wear Metro Authority (now Nexus); this building has transport associations going back a long way. The live electric rail is seen boxed in to offer some protection to track-walkers but note that in one place a boardwalk is sited right alongside the live rail.
A. R. Thompson Collection

Left: Thompson Class B1, No 61219, is seen shortly after Nationalisation crossing the Tyne near West Wylam with a Carlisle-Newcastle train. It sports the interim 'BRITISH RAILWAYS' legend on its tender; meanwhile a fisherman refuses to be distracted whilst tickling out a salmon as No 61219 rattles by overhead. The bridge remains today as part of a very good cycle/walk route from Newburn to Prudhoe whilst the route hugging the river behind continues to serve the Tyne valley via South Wylam.
J. W. Armstrong Trust Collection

Left: An austere working day setting is caught at Hebburn(-on-Tyne) station in June 1945 as a dour but inquisitive group of Geordies detrain from their South Shields-bound electric. The station furniture repays close study with its cable drum, pigeon baskets, etc.
J. W. Armstrong Trust Collection

Left: These were the lucky few who had found work (even for the day) at the peak of unemployment difficulties on Tyneside in 1936. They are being put to work replacing the conductor rail following alteration work on the 22 May. This is the southeast curve that led from Benton Station onto the ECML and thence Heaton, etc. In the background stands Benton Quarry signalbox, so named after the rocky outcrop blasted away here to facilitate the course of the main line. As with our other tracklaying view from about this time, the average age of these men is probably nearly 50, a far cry from today's working age profile when 50 is commonly retirement age. Again it is also interesting to note how headgear was a useful device in assessing a man's work related status. The 'bowlers' are obviously in charge but this time we have a bare-headed man who seems to be a tradesman joiner.
J. W. Armstrong Trust Collection

Left: There are 10 days to go prior to the 20 March 1933 opening of West Monkseaton station. The new station construction methods of this time show a clean finish. The anticipated expansion in housing in this coastal corridor was soon realised once the station was open.
E. Brack

Left: A view looking the other way, soon after the opening and in better weather. Note the preponderance of wood in every part of the construction.
E. Brack

Below: Another opportunity for civic dignitaries to launch a named train's career occurred 13 years later, this time for the first up run of the 'Tees-Tyne Pullman'. On 27 September 1948 'A1' No 60115, recently delivered new to Gateshead, prepares to leave as the new headboard is unveiled. Behind the guests a suspended signal gantry is fitted with miniature shunting arms. ***British Railways/Author's Collection***

Above: The inaugural down 'Silver Jubilee' is given a ceremonial send-off from Newcastle Central's Platform 8 by the Lord Mayor at 10am on 30 September 1935. ***Courtesy British Railways***

Below right: In June 1934 the LNER locomotive committee agreed to the construction of 90 new electric vehicles and to the renovation of the NER stock. A full board meeting soon after agreed to electrify the Newcastle-South Shields line and to work it with the renovated NER stock. This 1947 picture shows the result of those decisions. These new sets were delivered from Metro-Cammell during 1937. Their original livery of red and cream gave way to blue and grey during the war years and this set, seen leaving Pelaw, is in these colours, sporting the LNER lozenge in the centre of the body. They remained in service until 17 June 1967 when BR ceased electric workings on Tyneside. ***Hubert Foster/Ian Allan Library***

Right: A line-up of LNER express steam power in the immediate postwar years under the west end screen of the middle arch.

There is much fascinating detail here. On the left Class B16 No 1383 appears to have set off, while over on the far platform 'A4' No 4483 (later 60024) *Kingfisher* has arrived in wartime black dirt over its green livery. Sister engine No 4482 (later 60023) *Golden Eagle* carries lamps to indicate an express working and it seems reasonable to assume that it will take *Kingfisher's* train to the south. Fashions and the adverts of the day proliferate on both platforms — Newcastle Central was then very cluttered. Today's much cleaner lines help focus attention on the beauty of Dobson's design.
W. B Greenfield/NELPG Collection

Left: A rare glimpse of the west end bays in the 1930s, when platform 15 was still busy with passengers. The notice behind the lady advertises half-day excursions to Yorkshire destinations in an attempt to curb the depression in receipts. Over to the right of the tall policeman the 'Echo' billboard announces, 'Northeast Steel merger details'. Simply add Glen Miller and the 'Charleston' and you have the 1930s.
Courtesy Newcastle Evening Chronicle

Above right: A westbound train at Backworth, on the fringe of the city suburbs and old Blyth & Tyne metals, in 1948. The Nationalisation process was working in reverse to today's (1990s) situation, as the newly-formed BR went about renumbering engines inherited from the LNER, in this instance a Gresley 'V1' 2-6-2T (the majority of which were employed on Tyneside at one time or another). They were popular with Gateshead and Heaton men and it is good to hear that this class, previously completely ignored for preservation, may figure in the next plans of the 'A1' building team — if a popular enough choice.
No E7641 has its interim BR number and awaits 60000 being added for the final result. Even by 1948 standards this train is of vintage consist. The bridge behind is one of four in the vicinity carrying minerals down to Tyne staiths at Northumberland Dock. In this case it is the Backworth waggonway bridge. ***W. A. Camwell***

Above: Another view of the 1937 Metro-Cammell sets. They were designed under the guidance of Gresley and, as can be seen, were articulated upon LNER T8 bogies. The sliding doors made them quick and easy for station crowds and station management, but, as also illustrated here, meant the onus was on the passenger to detrain on the correct side! The position of adjacent doors above the bogie unfortunately encouraged a particular foolhardy element to 'coach-leap' en route! Amazingly there were only a handful of serious accidents. This view was captured at South Gosforth in their final full year of operation. The station buildings behind were erased in the mid-1970s to make way for a signalling centre for the Metro. ***Author***

Left: The result of 34 cars being destroyed by German aircraft at Heaton in 1918 was this Mark 2 NER design. Built at York Works between 1920 and 1922, the replacements included more modern curved roof designs against the clerestory of the older stock. The set here has the combined route and destination indicator adopted for the NER design and eventually standardised. This 1950 view shows the 'flying bridge' platform around the perimeter of No 1 Signalbox. It was frequently used to shout instructions to engine crew.
J. W. Armstrong Trust Collection

Right: Two views of *Kingfisher* at the head of a train needing no introduction — traditionally the 10am departure from King's Cross. In the first view, in 1939, it was signalled as train 384 and arrived at Newcastle at 2.33pm for a 3min stopover when, as can be seen, water for the engine was a priority. These were the last few weeks of the golden age of the LNER and these garter blue engines were never quite to fulfil their expectations as the thrust of modifications to fine-honed perfection was blocked by the war. The second view shows a de-valanced *Kingfisher,* now BR No 60024, in 1950, also snatching water time, but with the later style headboard including Scottish thistles in the motif. The whistle appears to be in use, perhaps to create some urgency — station overtime then being a subject of inquiry and copious reports.
W. B. Greenfield/ NELPG

Right: Not frequently seen by passing East Coast travellers was the railway activity below station height to the south of the goods lines, behind the large 140,000gal water tower of 1891. This area gave access to the Robert Stephenson Hawthorn works at Forth Banks via some tight curves. In this 1958 view the works' own crane tank has just crossed Forth Street into the infirmary sidings area with a 13-ton wagon. The west end gantry up at station level can just be glimpsed. ***D. G. Charlton***

Above: Rarely glimpsed or photographed, the end of the train in the 1930s was quite an interesting view and reflected the total imagery sought by LNER marketing experts. In what were dark days on Tyneside, the silver and blue of these new streamlined expresses gave something of a return to a feel-good factor to many. Even the imaginations of Gateshead housewives were captured by the hype and they would make a note of passing times, frequently turning out to view them. Low Fell provided an excellent vantage point, with not only the station but two bridges and further along an occupation crossing. Bryce Greenfield took full advantage of all the locations and such views are a tribute to his interest and creditable efforts to record a passing moment in the history of railways in the Northeast. ***W. B. Greenfield/NELPG***

Left: Under close scrutiny at the west end of Platform 9 in this mid-1930s view is 'A3' Pacific *Spearmint.*
W. B. Greenfield/NELPG

Left: Always an occasion anywhere was the arrival of a Pullman train, and especially at Newcastle, when engine and coaches were watered and checked out. On this occasion in 1938 the wheel-tapper is busy at the second coach, while sunlight streams in through the smoke patterns. 'A3' No 2578 *Bayardo* is in charge.
W. B. Greenfield/NELPG

Left: Interrupting progress on packing and general length maintenance at Platform 8 is 'A3' Pacific No. 2596 *Manna.* In Platform 7 NER stock forms a stopping service to Berwick.
W. B. Greenfield/NELPG

Right: Against an unfamiliar-looking backdrop of the south side end-screen, with buildings visible across Forth Street, Gresley 'A3' No 2795 *Call Boy*, later to become BR No 60099, is viewed by the camera from platform 10 while running through on the goods lines light engine, en route from Gateshead to Heaton sheds.
W. B. Greenfield/NELPG

Below: Another view of No 2795 *Call Boy* — this time at Gateshead Shed's east end watering position. A wagon intended for ash sits among spillages of the same and to the far left another 'A3' is receiving coal from the massive Gateshead coal stage. A metal oil can sits on the footplate, while a footplateman gives the cylinder head some attention. *Call Boy* saw regular duty on the north main line to Edinburgh.
W. B. Greenfield/NELPG

Left: Under the southern roof arch, adjacent to an area normally occupied by mail vans and short sets, is No 2597 (later 60040), *Cameronian,* another of Gresley's 1924 production batch. Oxo and Bainbridge's (department store) adverts relieve an otherwise bare back wall.
W. B. Greenfield/NELPG

Below: *Windsor Lad* (still remembered by some as the runaway winner of the 1934 Derby and St Leger) stands beneath the main arch at Central station, awaiting a down express to return to home — Edinburgh. No 2500 (later to become BR No 60035) was for most of its entire career based north of the Border, mostly at Haymarket Depot, Edinburgh. Withdrawn earlier than most of its Scottish brethren (1961), she was a frequent visitor to Central. No 2500 was the first of the final design batch of its class, completed in 1934.
W. B. Greenfield/NELPG

Above: Another view displaying the elegance of the main arch of Central's roof, and one that must also evoke many memories for those of us who witnessed the great Gresley age of the LNER in the 1930s. No 4490 was of the second production batch of Class A4 that went into traffic in June 1937, one year before this view. Retaining its original name *Empire of India* until the end (1964), it was at this time based at Edinburgh Haymarket, where it remained until 1962, before its final shed base, Aberdeen. Note the ornamental stainless steel strip along the lower edge of both the wheel valance and tender. No 4490 also had cut-out metal numerals and tender lettering, in tune with working the 'Coronation' express. It held the distinction of having hauled this service more times than any of its class before its demise on 31 August 1939. ***W. B. Greenfield/NELPG***

Right: This semi-silhouette taken into the sun at the west end shows vividly how the footboards on the signal posts could make life difficult for drivers in this particular lighting. Taking water on the goods road (far left), the driver of another Gresley design (a 'J39') looks on, perhaps a mite enviously, as *Empire of India* brings the down 'Flying Scotsman' through the maze of routes at this end of Central and into platform 9. The large No 3 Signalbox, hard up against the gable end of the Forth Goods Depot in the 'V', was originally sited opposite. It went with the 1959 changeover to electro-pneumatic signalling.

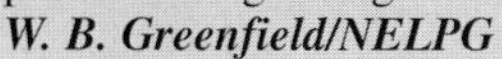

W. B. Greenfield/NELPG

118
Nº 240

DOMINION OF CANADA
Nº 4489

Above left: This view towards the east end of platform 10 shows a long-gone scene — barely recognisable when compared with the present day view. To the far left is the glass screen which gave passengers some protection from the cold winds whipped up off the river below but mainly there to support the glass canopy extension from the main train shed — well illustrated here. The outer wall is also on view; today this is a mid-point between the two through platforms. This is a rare view of the first Class A2 Pacific; regrettably the engine number cannot be identified. This Raven class was trialled against the emerging Gresley 'A3s' in what transpired to be unequal competition and was thus fated to a relatively short life-span of approximately 14 years. All five were withdrawn between 1936 and 1937. One of the class, No 2400, was named *City of Newcastle*. ***W. B. Greenfield/NELPG***

Below left: In the 1930s the north end of platform 8 was a popular location to record 'A4s' at a time when you were considered lucky if your camera had a top shutter speed of 125th of a second! Also with cut-out metal numbers and lettering for work on the 'Coronation' service, No 4489 (later BR No 60010) *Dominion of Canada* awaits departure on this celebrated express, while the fireman checks out coupling operations. No 4489 had been presented with the bell by the Canadian Government. In 1965 it was condemned for cutting up at Darlington and lay outside the shed until someone from the Canadian Government spotted and took pity on its forlorn condition (so the story goes…). One cosmetic refurbishment later, she went across the Atlantic (returning the bell!) on board MV *Beaverbrook* in April 1967 and is now on display in Canada's equivalent of our National Railway Museum at Montreal. ***W. B. Greenfield/NELPG***

Above: Rounding the final bend at Breckenbeds before the home straight into Gateshead is 'A4' No 4486 *Merlin* (later BR No 60027), at the head of one of the many and popular excursions once sponsored by the *Newcastle Evening Chronicle* during the interwar years. The immaculate state of the cess between fast and slow lines is worthy of note; it is said to have been at the behest of the Chief Area Engineer, John Millar. The career of No 60027 lasted from April 1937 until September 1965, when it went for breaking up near the shipyards at Shieldhall in Glasgow. Its metals may, therefore, live on, albeit unrecognisably — roaming the oceans of the world! ***W. B. Greenfield/NELPG***

Above: Another view of the down (northbound) 'Flying Scotsman' as it cautiously eases round the tight curves onto the King Edward Bridge, on the approach to Newcastle from the 'valley' (as local railwaymen still call the 'new' Team Valley route). The attention to detail in presenting the best possible image to the traveller passing through a slightly grim location is well illustrated in the area behind the engine. Today it has returned to an untidy eyesore complete with electric substation. The engine is No 2578 (later 60079) *Bayardo*. It spent much of its career in the Tyneside and Carlisle area, going to scrap from Heaton Shed in October 1962 — an early casualty of dieselisation. ***W. B. Greenfield/NELPG***

Below: A fine study of an 'A4' — and looking as Gresley had intended.. This example, No 4497 *Golden Plover* (BR No 60031) is seen switching from up fast to up slow lines at Low Fell station approach in 1938. No 4497 was always a Scottish engine. It moved down from regular East Coast duties to trans-Scottish expresses in 1962, when many of the class were being withdrawn. Its own Indian summer lasted until October 1965; these extra years of running in places like Glenfarg and Gleneagles were a joy to the many Gresley devotees who had begun taking summer holidays in Scotland. The coaching stock in this view is certainly worth another glance. ***W. B. Greenfield/NELPG***

4

Towards Modernisation (1949-1962)

Polkadots and Perry Como may have been the big find of the 1950s but the popularisation of the internal combustion engine was not lost upon the new-look railways now governed in pseudo-military style by the British Transport Commission at No 222 Marylebone Road, London. In 1948 Newcastle and the the East Coast route in this area became part of the North Eastern Region of British Railways and the Regional headquarters was the old NER Main HQ building at York — some things, at least, never change.

To get a feeling for the 1950s at Newcastle, let us look back to the delightful Ian Allan *Trains Illustrated* magazine of the time. It ran an occasional in-depth article on a large centre of activity in those days. In the May 1958 edition that railway researcher extraordinaire, Brian Perren, filled eight pages under the title of 'Resorts for Railfans No 24 — Newcastle Central'. Take then a glimpse into the world of 1957-8 and let us start by looking at some general comments by Brian:

'The railway geography of the Newcastle area is somewhat complex because of its many alternative routes, flat junctions, intermediate signalboxes and stations. Approaching Newcastle from the south, the main line from Durham and York is joined at King Edward Bridge Signalbox by the route from Blaydon and Consett via Dunston, and the latter throws off a connection to give its trains access to the King Edward Bridge. The main line then divides into a double track, curving sharply leftwards onto the bridge, and another double track — the old entry into Newcastle — continues past Gateshead motive power depot and works, paralleled by the two Dunston tracks as far as Greensfield [sic] box. A fourth double track from Greensfield box onto the bridge completes the triangle, and two of the three junctions are controlled by Greensfield box.'

He continues:

'The High Level Bridge, over which there are three tracks... [which] converge on the famous manganese steel crossing with two pairs of tracks from Manors, both of which are electrified; they are respectively the up and down North main lines. No 1 signalbox is in command of operations at this end of Central station and the east end of the goods lines. The use of manganese has increased

Text continues on page 54

Right: One benefit of the electro-pneumatic signalling of 1959 was the ability to introduce a 'control' aspect into the new centralised power signalbox. Newcastle had a back-desk rostrum located where a supervisor could easily oversee the passage of trains and guide the signalmen in matters of regulation. This was a plum job compared to the hours of standing by those 'on the panel.' To the extreme left is the glass, sound-proofed office where the station announcers where located. A glance by them at the tracery of lights and they could time their arrival announcements to perfection. ***British Railways Board/ J. W. Armstrong Trust Collection***

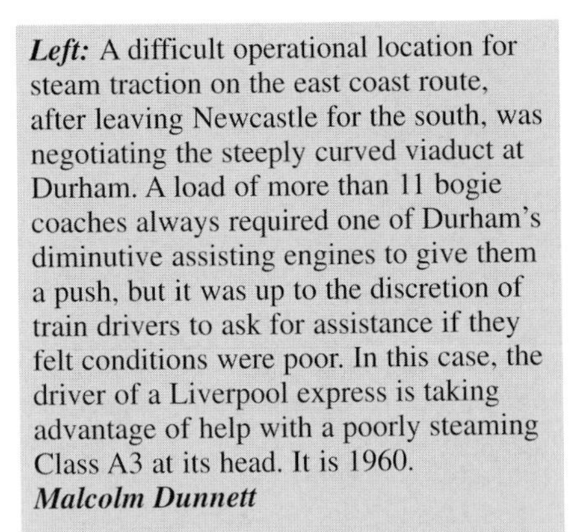

Left: A difficult operational location for steam traction on the east coast route, after leaving Newcastle for the south, was negotiating the steeply curved viaduct at Durham. A load of more than 11 bogie coaches always required one of Durham's diminutive assisting engines to give them a push, but it was up to the discretion of train drivers to ask for assistance if they felt conditions were poor. In this case, the driver of a Liverpool express is taking advantage of help with a poorly steaming Class A3 at its head. It is 1960.
Malcolm Dunnett

Left: South Shields station today continues (if in part only) to provide facilities to Metro travellers and this branch has a long history connected to electric traction in its many forms. Elsewhere both NER (1904) and Eastleigh (1955) EMU sets are illustrated which at one time supplied Shields people with their rail propulsion. The South Shields to Sunderland service was never electrified and remained steam-hauled until the advent of DMUs in the late 1950s. Class G5 No 67247 carries the contradiction of a British Railways number below an LNER decal in 1948 — perhaps the painter was interrupted!
W. A. Camwell

Right: The British Railways look: this was the final form of the engine that still holds the world speed record for steam traction. A common sight at Newcastle during the 1940s and '50s, *Mallard's* record of 126mph is a modest top speed when considering the cruise speed of 125mph by the electric trains that now pass Central.
British Railways Board

Above: Another engine to frequent these parts, *W. P. Allen* demonstrated to all engine drivers that they too could aspire to great things with the right momentum — and perhaps a little good fortune! W. P. Allen began life as an engine cleaner on the old Great Northern. He became involved in the waiting game known as 'shed links', ie promotion based upon seniority. Allen, however, became concerned in fighting for his fellow workers as their trade union representative and having sat across the table from the top brass, impressed the latter so much that he eventually made it onto the executive committee of the British Transport Commission. A happy thought concerning this class of loco — 'A1' — is that although none survived to be preserved, a new engine to this design is currently being built and, hopefully, will be seen passing Newcastle again around the time of the millennium celebrations. ***British Railways***

Above: Designed by Gresley and built in Doncaster in 1934 as a 'P2', No 2001 was rebuilt into the form seen here under Thompson in 1944 and subsequently was experimented upon, in an effort to improve performance. It frequently ran to Newcastle from the north in the 1940s. In the 1950s it was mainly York-based and after a very mixed career ended its days in 1960, after only 16 years of service since rebuilding. This illustration shows the loco in the all-black wartime livery in September 1944, with tablet exchange apparatus on the tender for single line sections in Scotland. Renumbered 60501 by BR, she was classified 'A2/2'.
British Railways

Above: An early 1950s view across the east end bays shows the Alnmouth stopping service making a sedate departure with Class D20 (known to enginemen as 'Rs') No 62396 at the head. These engines had been cascaded down to minor duties by this time but the authorities were reluctant to dispose of them completely, due to their popularity and reliability. For engines that first appeared in 1899 to the design of Wilson Worsdell, their survival on passenger duties until 1957 in this area is a great tribute to the workmanship of Gateshead Works. They became the NER's 'fliers' in the early 1900s, holding the blue riband for hauling the fastest train in the Empire (the 12.20pm Newcastle-Bristol express) until 1914. No 62396 was one of the final six to be withdrawn, from Alnmouth shed in 1957. ***J. W. Armstrong Trust Collection***

Above: An engine that features elsewhere, but this particular study illustrates the sleek racing form of the Gresley 'A3' Pacifics. Named *Call Boy* after the racehorse that won the 1927 Derby, it spent an unprecedented 32 years based in Scotland, never south of the border. However, Newcastle saw much of No 2795 during its life-span of 1930-1963, as a regular with express services to and from Edinburgh. ***British Railways***

Right: The early 1950s saw the area still grey and war-ravaged, with the dregs of rationing continuing to enforce a frugal lifestyle. The railway was particularly badly hit and the shine of late-1930s achievements was lost for ever, amid scenes such as this, where a tired and dirty 'A4', once resplendent in blue, would very often struggle to keep time with only 300 tons trailing weight. Gateshead-based *Bittern* heads the London-bound 'Flying Scotsman' on 30 July 1952, in a pre-computer game world where entertainment was a hole in the fence adjacent to the King Edward Bridge! ***British Railways***

Right: Workhorses meet on the main line at Durham. Class Q6 came to typify slogging reliability and was dependable where no slow lines or refuge sidings existed. In this view No 63384 has cleared the viaduct with mineral supplies for West Durham pitland, while sister No 63431 brings coals to Newcastle, or more precisely, to Tyneside's power station complex at Stella, near Blaydon. It is June 1961. ***Alan R. Thompson***

Left: On the fringes of Tyneside, steam hung on into the early 1950s, before the advent of diesel multiple-units completely usurped all their passenger duties for ever. Hexham shed, nestling in a particularly pleasant part of the Tyne Valley, had various steam duties up and down the various Tyne Valley lines surrounding. In this 1955 view, the tender of a 'J21' can be seen at the back of the shed, while meat containers line the up refuge sidings beyond. These were the dying moments for this way of life, as outbased engine crews became a rarity and centralisation at big depots heralded the style of things to come. ***J. W. Armstrong Trust Collection***

Left: There was no way a book concerning Newcastle was going to appear without a football reference somewhere! After looking at this picture (and in view of recent events at St James' Park) many might question if we may see these scenes ever again — including the 'A1'! 1951 was the beginning of what is still considered by many as the Magpies' heyday and this year was to be the first of three famous victories that were to make the cup 'wors'. As can be seen here, the railway authorities entered into the spirit of the celebration and No 60126 *Sir Vincent Raven* stands suitably dressed to take the conquering heroes home to Newcastle for the start of celebrations that were to last weeks. The Gateshead engineman looks unmoved (could he be a Sunderland supporter, I wonder?) as he gives No 60126 the final once-over at York station on 3 May 1951. ***British Railways***

Centre left: Low Fell station, now reduced to a trackworker's house with platforms removed, gently shakes as one of Riddles massive Class 9s powers by in typically filthy condition. It is Sunday morning and the Washington section of the Consett-Tyne Dock line is probably closed for maintenance, thus forcing this empty ore train to travel back via Low Fell and Felling and also ensuring that the Tyne Dock crew retain route knowledge over this, the normal diversion alternative. In the right background is Low Fell sidings.
A. R. Thompson

Below left: A 'B16' in third-rail territory, June 1955. Stars of David dominate the canopy detail of this Heaton view, which also shows the steps leading up to the access point off Heaton Road. Heaton was an excellent place to await electric trains and, tantalisingly, movements from the shed area in the distance would often reach the far signal gantry and return to the shed — just out of number-sighting distance! This 'B16' had, presumably, brought an Anglo-Scottish goods load into Heaton goods yards and was offered no more than one paltry engineer's wagon in return. Not so common north of Newcastle, the presence of 'B16s' hereabouts eventually receded more and more as they remained within Yorkshire boundaries, with only occasional sorties north of York by the late 1950s. Not a trace of Heaton's platforms survive today and Metro trains sweep up the remaining commuters on a parallel course through Byker.
A. R. Thompson Collection

Above: The view from the long overbridge that linked Manors North and East (main line) platforms. Platform 7, on the up slow, was used by city commuters working in the New Bridge Street and Northumberland Road area of Newcastle. The exit from Manors brought them out into Carlisle Square and the curious resting place for Northern buses soaking up time between duties. Today this area is part of a central area motorway that also removed much of Picton Place. The electric loco is taking current via its pick-up shoes from the third-rail. It is on its way back to South Gosforth sheds after a day's shunting on the quayside branch nearby; 9 September 1961. ***Ian S. Carr***

Above: The end of steam on passenger work along the rural west line to Hexham and Carlisle came with the arrival of these units working from South Gosforth car sheds. This example, in the Newburn/Blaydon area, shows off the overall dark BR green livery with lion & wheel insignia. Permanent way staff were warned they were 'silent and deadly' on a poster with a cheetah to underline the theme. Their arrival pushed Standard Class 4 and 5 engines back onto freight work, some being transferred out of the area, and caused a reduction in 'V' tanks. ***J. W. Armstrong Trust Collection***

Left: This view from 1962 makes for an interesting comparison with the scene taken 10 years earlier of *Bittern* working the 'Flying Scotsman'. The engine of the same name, and perhaps the most famous steam locomotive in the world, was not frequently seen as far north as Newcastle, as King's Cross engines were mostly out and home Doncaster or York (with some overnight exceptions). On this occasion No 60103, in its final BR form with German-style smoke deflectors, leads the midday Newcastle-Bristol train into County Durham. Already an old lady of almost 30 years, she was withdrawn six months afterwards, and the rest is history. She resides today, in kit form pending major surgery, at Southall under her new and third owner since BR days, Dr Tony Marchington. **Peter J. Robinson**

Left: A picture such as this is perhaps how most of us would like to remember steam in the 1950s Better known to enthusiasts then as 'streaks', the 'A4s'' syncopated three-cylinder beat plus nasal-sounding Kylchap blastpipe was good music. The difficulty in lifting 300 tons off Platform 10's curve and out over the King Edward Bridge caused some particularly fine music that lingered on in the air for some time, leaving the senses somewhat arrested and unwilling to move on. No 60017 *Silver Fox*, showing its shed as 34A (King's Cross), was the last of the original 'silver four'. Withdrawn in October 1963, it had only two shed bases, King's Cross and New England, in its 28 years. **Peter J. Robinson**

service between renewals, the last of which occurred in 1956, when a 1949 set was taken out; it will be replaced when the present layout requires refettling. The two layouts (one spare) are prefabricated and are first assembled at the manufacturer's works for checking, then dismantled and taken to Low Fell Storeyard for transfer to the site.'

While describing the platform arrangement at Central, he makes a mention of the goods lines thus:

'Beyond the wall adjoining these sidings are the four goods lines which avoid the station itself but not the busy crossings at either end. The west-end carriage dock is used for loading parcels and miscellaneous goods, including the weekend theatrical traffic, horses and, during summer, cars for the Car-Sleeper service.'

Referring to the signalling, which was at that time in a transitional state, Brian mentions the pedigree of the previous era:

'Electro-pneumatic operation of the points and signals was installed by the North Eastern Railway in 1909 and one of the features of the scheme was the operation from No 3 Signalbox of the massive gantry at the west end, which had 57 arms on 25 posts, later modified to 43 arms on 16 posts, and was one of the largest in the country. No 3 Box is sited beyond the junctions at the west end...It has a large frame of miniature levers manned by three signalmen, assisted by two "book" lads, while a traffic regulator supervisors the working. The boxes on either side are King Edward Bridge, Forth Junction, No 2 — in the station — and No 1 at the east end of the goods lines.'

Moving on from the technical aspects, Brian nicely sums up the nature of 1950s traffic:

Right: South Gosforth Car Sheds. The depot is on the Ponteland branch spur, just round the corner from South Gosforth station. These car sheds were opened in 1923 and replaced the earlier steam depot on this site. The latter itself replaced the very early New Bridge Street shed of the Blyth & Tyne in 1902. It is now taken over by Tyneside PTE for the maintenance of its Metro stock. This August 1958 view shows the west end and the small office block that once included the Running Foreman's office. A Met-Cam EMU set is poking out of the shed while DMUs sit along the south wall holding area. They were to oust the EMUs completely by 1967. ***J. W. Armstrong Trust Collection***

Right: The 1954 city view from the long overbridge then straddling the apex of the two Gateshead stations. Not only an excellent vantage point to stand and breathe in the heady cocktail of river sounds and smells (!) as if on some kind of industrial viewing platform, but also close enough to Gateshead Shed to get the full health benefits of acrid steam, hot ash and the odd sulphurous blast from the ash pit roads that lay just over your left shoulder. Conversely, and what frequently drove one off this magnificent perch, were the tantalising glimpsed sleek Pacific shapes coming and going at the far end of the bridge. The choice was then to walk the High Level Bridge lower deck to Central, or walk Askew Road to King Edward Bridge South Junction — a difficult choice to make! As seen here, a 'V3' hauling a semi-fast to Middlesbrough did much to relieve the numerous electric sets shuttling up and down to 'Sheels'. In this instance it is No 67634 plus seven coaches.
J. W. Armstrong Trust Collection

Right: The post-1952 age saw the end of semaphores over the High Level Bridge and a small colour-light makes for a poor visual replacement of that which went before. The preponderance of timber, in what is essentially a huge wooden platform to build up the junction here, resulted in frequent smoulderings after the passage of an engine off Gateshead shed. At least this relatively new Eastleigh built electric set posed no threat. It is about to cross the walkway between the platforms ends to enter East station with a South Shields 'stopper'. ***J. W. Armstrong Trust Collection***

Left: The NER had been eager to partake of the success of others, when the opportunity arose, at its installations along the Tyne. Here at Albert Edward Dock, North Shields, the 1930s addition of deep water berthing with passenger embarkation for Scandinavia had given the NER a chance to connect its passenger services to holidays abroad as it had done so at Hull. The large shed in the murk is the Bergen Line transit shed at Tyne Commission Quay into which the NER had running rights, for through London trains. Goods traffic, however, — and vehicle exports especially — still eclipsed passengers receipts when this photograph was taken in August 1954.
John Johnson/J. W. Armstrong Trust Collection

Left: Many NER lines made contact directly onto the Tyne river-front via the Quayside link to the Manors area. This one traversed the new corporation (concrete) quay extension of 1954. This enabled Spillers food products to be conveyed to the Forth Goods station for onward distribution. Raw materials (flour) invariably arrived by way of vessels such as *Baron Renfrew* for discharge via the 'spiders legs' suction equipment. 1957.
John Johnson/J. W. Armstrong Trust Collection

'Passenger traffic falls into certain broad divisions: residential local electric services to Tynemouth and South Shields, and steam to Newbiggin: medium distance passenger DMUs to Middlesbrough and Carlisle: and long-distance express services by the East Coast route. The South Shields service was not electrified until 1938 and makes an 11-mile run. It takes the High Level route as far as Pelaw, whence it leaves the main line to Sunderland, to make for Hebburn, Jarrow and Tyne Dock. Both the Tynemouth and South Shields cars are based on Gosforth Sheds, although certain sets stable away from the depot at various times.'

Brian continues to describe the changing vehicles that have serviced the South Shields branch through to the then-current use of the Eastleigh sets of 1951 origin, and then enters into much detail concerning the employment of DMUs. It seems strange amid so much high technology and brand-new units, that when he moves on to the most important trains of the day on the East Coast route he refers to the importance of steam, and it is here we get the message that, although technology is creeping ahead and the genre of English Electric is already on the horizon, Gresley products still command the scene for power and reliability — just!

'The most important main line steam services are the passenger trains over the East Coast route. With the sole but noteworthy exception of the King's Cross-Edinburgh non-stop

Above: With shed code 54C, Borough Gardens could hold upwards of 80 engines and often had to when the main shed at Gateshead had problems and was overflowing! A shunting loco, No 68736, keeps company with a larger and more powerful heavy freight locomotive, Class Q6 No 63456, photographed c1958.

In 1963 this became the site of the Tyneside Central Freight Depot with easy access onto the Felling by-pass. Eldon Street Goods (opposite) was incorporated into the Tyneside Central Freight Depot. Today, in 1998, the TCFD lies languishing and vandalised awaiting its next role. ***F. W. Hampson***

Left: With shed code 52C, Blaydon locomotive depot was within an elongated triangle bounded by the river, Chain Bridge Road, the Scotswood branch and the station itself at the narrowest angle. It was therefore particularly suited for its engines to access the majority of lines radiating to the west of Newcastle, including Consett. The classes on display (left to right) 'J39', 'G5' and 'Q6' were typical for the shed's requirements in the 1950s. ***F. W. Hampson***

Left: A view outside the main shed building at Blaydon. Another example of its Class J39 allocation moves into the sunlight for its next duty. The small office-block seen under construction in this 1959 view is still extant and is today the Co-op dairy.
F. W. Hampson

Left: South of Durham, at a place where Consett traffic could once access the main East Coast line for the south, was Relly Mill. We see, on Sunday 17 July 1960, a 'Q6', No 63448, awaiting the right away with a train load of steel plate from Consett. Although it appears in this view that the diesel is a southbound express on the main line, it is in fact taking the Bishop Auckland road. It is a planned diversion as the engineer has the main line under an engineering possession this day.
Ian S. Carr

Left: Relly Mill Junction, south of Durham, was even more complex when viewed to the south. Even though technically still Relly Mill, this junction was known as Deerness Valley Junction and had the added complication of the Waterhouses branch tapering in from the north. This is the view from Relly Mill towards Bishop Auckland as EE Type 4 1Co-Co1 No D259 does some propelling to avoid an engineering possession with a down freight on 19 June 1960.
Robert Leslie

Left: The region's railways continued to be starved of cash throughout the 1950s until the modernisation programme — resurrected in 1955 — began to have some effect, with mass steam withdrawals from the late 1950s onwards. A snapshot of the real operating conditions on Tyneside as late as 1958, can be glimpsed in this view outside Heaton locomotive shed where much needed track maintenance work had to be done 'between trains' in circumstances that were fraught with danger and took an age to complete satisfactorily. Class ES1 electric loco No 26501 sets off from the shed for its afternoon shift on the Quayside branch. ***Malcolm Dunnett***

Right: The mass withdrawal campaign begun in the 1950s saw Darlington North Road scrapyard kept busy right through to 1964 when the policy altered and the scrapping of engines went out to contract. An engine seen in the Newcastle area from time to time was Class G5 No 67293. Built at Darlington in 1897, this was also to be its last resting place in 1955. The class was extinct by December 1958 but it had been remarkably resilient to change in its longevity, seeing Britain through two world wars. ***Bob Payne***

Left: At the start of the day's work, a 'J72' would accompany the 'ES1' electric from Heaton down to the Quayside Goods station and await instructions. After approximately 1960, the reduced work load reduced the need for the steam engine and the electric would often work alone between the Quay and Trafalgar Yard. This mid-1950s picture demonstrates some of the 'navigational' problems associated with shunting in less 'dedicated' railway circumstances! The engine, a Class J72 from Heaton, No 69024, has recessed a tank wagon whilst awaiting for an Austin A30 van to be moved.
L. G. Charlton/A. R. Thompson

Left: NER and LNER electric units line up here at South Gosforth in April 1960. It seems all the more surprising from our 1990s viewpoint that some of the older, wooden-bodied passenger stock was retained into the 1960s. The reason they were retained is interesting; they became 'perambulator vehicles' and thus were wheeled out to assist with the summer-day mass exodus of Tynesiders to the coastal stations. Prams were quite a problem in the days when they had wheels almost as big as the trains themselves! The last retained for this reason was withdrawn two years later, in 1962.
N. Skinner/J. W. Armstrong Trust Collection

"Elizabethan", all of them stop at Newcastle Central…It is possible to travel by through service to such varied destinations as Colchester, Cardiff, Bristol, Manchester and Liverpool, as well as important intermediate centres on the route of these trains, such as Sheffield and Leeds…'

A modern day comparison shows how we are now offered many more route destinations, even though the railway of today is post-Beeching. The 1950s and 1960s railway was very much one of tradition and repetition. Some changes were made to tweak early morning business trains as habits altered, and dieselisation meant a return to postwar speeds into the capital but elsewhere there was little incentive, perhaps because there was no call, for new destinations. Specials or excursions were the main tester of a public that was still attracted to rail travel but was becoming seriously diverted by the now trendy looking little Morris and Austin family cars in colours other than black.

However, BR anticipated the car and also, in this pre-motorway age, saw the value of car-trains for the longer route with the mid-1950s introduction of the Anglo-Scottish car carrier and the forerunner of the Motorail services that, sadly, have been a casualty of privatisation.

Another less recent loss to the East Coast route was the sleeping car train. Newcastle businessmen once had a wide sweep of destinations available to them, but, again, habits change. Brian tells us that:

'During the night the station is busy with the now expanding service of sleeping car trains. The first of these to be dealt with is the 10.55pm "Tynesider" for King's Cross, which starts from Newcastle: only sleeping car passengers are now conveyed by this train. The first down sleeping car train to arrive is the 07.45pm from King's Cross with coaches for Elgin, Aberdeen and Fort William. The new 10.15pm "Aberdonian" and the 11.35pm "Night Scotsman" from King's Cross stop only to change engines, but the 7.45pm from London detaches newspaper traffic; also in the up direction, the 8.35pm from Aberdeen and the 10.50pm from Edinburgh stop only for locomotive purposes.'

A feature of these days was the high number of passengers who were prepared to travel through the night 'on the cushions' and many trains were formed up and run for this purpose, with enginemen's lodging turns designed for these non-stops to the capital. Brian lists the choice of trains available then:

'The departures from Newcastle are at 1.3, 1.18 and 2.52am. There are similar down departures (from London for Tyneside) at 10.15, 11.20 and 11.35pm.'

Moving on, we next learn what the main events of the day were:

'The first important day train is the 8.0am to King's Cross, worked through by Gateshead men to London, where it is due at 1.15pm. The through day trains to and from Scotland, with one exception apart from the summer "Elizabethan", all change engines at Newcastle. A Gateshead engine works the 6.40am from York to Edinburgh throughout,

Left: Caught hard at work in Quayside yard in 1956 is ESII electric loco No 26500. It is seen taking juice from the catenary in the yard prior to moving a rake of wagons up through the semi-circular tunnel to Trafalgar Yard. This loco is now part of the National Collection at York NRM. ***J. W. Armstrong Trust Collection***

Left: The fire-damaged remains of Bowes Bridge engine shed (a sub-shed of Gateshead) seen in 1955. The incumbent Class N10 engines may have been any of half-a-dozen out-based here at this time. The current shed of today's Tanfield Railway is behind the photographer's position. ***J. W. Armstrong Trust Collection***

although its diagram starts with an early train from Newcastle to York. Newcastle is unique in that all main motive power depots between Edinburgh and London have workings to Tyneside. On arrival at Newcastle engines of down arrivals uncouple and, according to their next working, either run over the High Level Bridge to Gateshead, where they turn on the Greensfield [sic] Junction triangle, or head out to Heaton. Engines coming off shed run up light from Heaton, or from Gateshead via the High Level or King Edward Bridges. For an up train, the engine will either wait on the KEB near No 3 Signalbox until the incoming engine has detached or, if the train is late, run into the sidings between the through platforms and known as "A-B sidings".'

Brian moves on to discuss the named trains of the day.

'King's Cross shed uses "A1s", "A3s" and "A4" Pacifics on its Newcastle turns, which include most of the faster trains such as the "Tees-Tyne Pullman" and the "Fair Maid" in both directions, the down "Talisman" and the fast 5.5pm up… Rosters are too intricate to be included in full and only the more important trains can be mentioned. Haymarket powers the up "Fair Maid" and the down train at 12.33pm, also the up "Talisman" due in at 6.7pm. Two other similar workings are the up Glasgow due at 1.22pm, returning with the down train at 3.25pm, and the up and down "Heart of Midlothian", due at 3.47pm and returning north at 6.15pm. A number of night trains are worked by Haymarket, but only one engine has two round trips to Newcastle in a day; this is the "Fair Maid" engine, which also covers the 10.50pm from Waverley and the 1.10am back from Newcastle.

'The "Flying Scotsman" and the "North Briton" are covered by Gateshead engines in each direction, while Heaton powers the "Queen of Scots". The longest distance train is the 312-mile through service to Cardiff.

Left: Gateshead shed yard on a strangely quiet Sunday morning. The main repair shed dominates the background of this rather fine portrait of King's Cross 'top-shed' engine No 60017 *Silver Fox.* It is being prepared for working back home on the 10.35 service from Newcastle. Evidently, several things, such as winding shut the smokebox door are still to be done — note the shed clock. Many years of use has resulted in the metals almost disappearing from sight!
A. R. Thompson

Left: This was a time when fuel tanks where more for lubrication than for the internal combustion engine (see extreme left). This time an interior view of a much older portion of the shed complex where steam-powered belts adorn the perimeter wall — one is still connected in this 1962 picture. Apple green-liveried Class J72, No 68723, stands alongside later sister No 69025 in this sleepy corner. Note that No 68723's shed plate has taken a heavy blow at some point!
A. R. Thompson

Left: In a rare view Alan Thompson has captured the green Class J72 at the point where the tracks led down towards Stephenson's works in South Street. The bulk of the south-facing wall can be seen — today it has a platform built outside it. ***A. R. Thompson***

Liverpool is served by four daily through trains leaving at 8.55am via Harrogate, 10.5 via the [Durham] coast, 4.15pm via the coast and Harrogate, and the 5.10pm via York.

'Arrivals from Liverpool are at 1.40, 4.18, 7.0 and 9.59pm. Two train sets, both with refreshment facilities, stable at either end of the service; the two Liverpool trains are of LM stock, while the two NE sets stable at Scotswood Bridge and Heaton. There is one interesting working in the Liverpool service — the 4.18 arrival, which stays in the Central station to form the 5.15pm back and is therefore the only long distance steam train using the station which does not go out of the station to sidings for servicing.'

Brian rounds off with details of the freight activities and the operational control in this area. He mentions in some detail the different work of the engines of the two main sheds, Heaton and Gateshead. It comes as quite a surprise to find that at this time Heaton had a larger number of engines than Gateshead, 102 to 83. He tells us that the range of diagrams worked by Gateshead was wider than those of Heaton, since the former covered the whole of the East Coast route and the men worked through to both Edinburgh and London. Although he fails to give us a blow by blow account of the situation on the platform through the day, we do at least understand from this account the complex nature of the very labour-intensive railway machine and get an inkling of just how poor, compared to today's every-hour service to London, was the main express service as recently as 1958. At Central station offices alone in those days there were 300 clerks and managers employed on the background work to keep the wheels turning. Of these, some 50 people would have been involved with diagrams, rosters and support work for the 560 train crews signing on and off all around the clock.

The railway was now ripe for paring down and, as with the Edwardian changeover to electro-pneumatic signalling, other technology, especially some already in use in the USA, was begging for installation over here. A Conservative Government with Ernest Marples as Transport supremo made it clear that BR must shape up and that investment in modern equipment would only come at the expense of loss-making rural routes and labour intensive activities (such as maintaining steam). Marples appointed Dr Beeching to execute the paring-down process.

Described by the late Gerry Fiennes, once General Manager of the Eastern Region, as 'the great and good Doctor', love him or hate him, Beeching did his job and the Eastern Region, of which the North Eastern Region was now a part, got new goods depots, marshalling yards and more diesel power to completely usurp the last fragments of steam.

Sunday 12 April 1959 saw the end of the old signalling system at Newcastle and the commissioning of the power signalling incorporating colour lights, route relay interlocking and compressed air operated pointwork. It also brought the work of four separate signalboxes into a new control room signalbox situated above and between old platforms 9 and 10. Under the new box's control passed 13 switch diamond crossings.

On most summer Saturdays over 340 suburban electric trains, 420 steam and diesel main line and suburban trains and some 80 freight movements used the lines controlled by this new box. In the morning peak period 51 trains would leave Central within an hour.

Left: Newcastle's west end as seen from the famous spotters' wall just above Forth Backlane, this position was a veritable viewing balcony. On show this fine day was Class G5, No 67265, leaving with a Hexham local train in the early 1950s. Behind stands the works of Robert Stephenson & Hawthorns, builders of many fine engines until closure in 1961.
Bob Payne

Below: Borough Gardens shed c1955. Class Q6, No 63354, a long-time resident of the shed, is seen with the depot's two Class B1s — used on the Park Lane-York fitted freights. On summer Saturdays these 'B1s' were often lent to a busy Gateshead shed, frequently for deployment to such places as Scarborough.
K. H. Cockerill/A. R. Thompson Collection

Above: Class D30 No 62432 *Quentin Durward* of Hawick stands in front of Blaydon shed's coaling stage, c1952-3. It would no doubt have arrived with the morning Hawick-Newcastle train and will return with the teatime working from Newcastle. Also to be seen in the background is Class J21, No 65090, a regular at Blaydon for many years. ***K. H. Cockerill/A. R. Thompson Collection***

Right: Backworth NCB, c1952/3, showing No 4, a Robert Stephenson product (works No 2232) of 1875 for the NER and one of their '964' class. It was purchased by the colliery in December 1889 and was withdrawn in November 1960 after having received a 'Backworth'-style cab plus quite a bit of history! ***K. H. Cockerill/ A. R. Thompson Collection***

Left: A 'captured' 'V3' tank in more ways than one, this engine had been 'borrowed' by the loco department at Heaton whilst en route via Darlington works to Glasgow, and pushed into a few small jobs around Tyneside to 'thoroughly test it'. Its home shed in Glasgow would, no doubt, have wondered why it took several weeks to eventually return home but this was nevertheless in a time-honoured tradition and deemed a fair cop — by the local 'spotters too! Here, No 67662 is caught by Alan Thompson taking the now empty set of a King's Cross train out of Tyne Commission Quay and back to Heaton carriage sidings. The Bergen Line transit shed behind was the link with the Norwegian Mail steamers which berthed alongside the tall cranes to the right. ***A. R. Thompson***

Above: *The Railway Observer* gave a tantalisingly short report in August 1959 simply stating that the GWR No 3440, *City of Truro* had been seen going north along the West Coast route. Then on 29 September 1959 it startled Tynesiders by appearing in Central station in the middle of the morning peak (causing quite a few to be late at office and school). It eventually came out that it had been guesting at the Glasgow 'Scottish Industries Fair' shortly after being put back into traffic by Swindon works and was thus returning to Swindon via the east coast route under its own steam. ***I. W. Coulson/A. R. Thompson Collection***

Above: About eight miles north of Newcastle was Killingworth station, seen in the summer of 1952. The station relied heavily upon local villages of Burradon, Camperdown and Weetslade to make up its passenger receipts. The name Killingworth has long associations in railway lore due to its connection with George Stephenson and his experimentation with engines on the early local waggonways. Class K3 , No 61984 of Heaton, is a long way along the evolution process from those far off days of the Killingworth engine. It is lifting a staged Heaton load onward to Edinburgh Yards. This is another location difficult to identify from the window one of today's speeding electric trains. ***J. W. Armstrong Trust Collection***

Left: This time from the footbridge, on the same day as the previous picture, the photographer has turned 180° and looks north to capture an Alnwick stopping service in the capable old hands of a Class D20, still on the fast track but now cascaded down to semi-fast trains. The very open cab of a previous age was not so popular with local crews by the 1950s, especially when the north wind blew. ***J. W. Armstrong Trust Collection***

Above: An engine named after its designer — *A. H. Peppercorn* — the prototype Class A2, No 60525 is seen here. A fairly rare sighting in this area, No 60525, an Aberdeen-based engine, powers over the diamond crossing area with the York-Edinburgh train in the winter of 1962, smoke and steam obscuring the Royal Station Hotel behind. It is interesting to note that this may have been its last working visit to Tyneside as soon afterwards, in March 1963, it blew the cover off of its middle cylinder and was withdrawn. ***A. R. Thompson***

Below: The final form in the evolution of the Gresley A3 Pacifics included German-style wind deflectors or 'blinkers'. Standing in Platform 9 is King's Cross (34A) No 60110 *Robert the Devil*, recently ex-works after having them fitted. It is at the head of an up King's Cross express and apparently under close scrutiny. It is July 1961. ***Jack Teasdale/T. J. Ermel Collection***

Left: A King's Cross-allocated Class A4, No 60025 *Falcon*, has just uncoupled from the down 'Talisman' express and heads off to Gateshead depot for servicing, via the High Level Bridge. The corridor tender is shown to good advantage in this view — an addition that allowed these streamliners to operate nonstop and still facilitate a crew change on the closely-timed and prestigious London-Edinburgh trains of the 1940s and 1950s. ***Jack Teasdale/ T. J. Ermel Collection***

Above: Moments later No 60025 was replaced by sister engine, No 60004 *William Whitelaw*, for the final leg of the journey to Edinburgh. Very much in keeping with the tradition at Haymarket No 4 is well turned-out; the station shunter gives the thumbs up sign to indicate that the buckeye coupling pin has dropped into position before connecting the train heating and brake pipes. This every day occurrence in the early 1960s was perhaps taken for granted by many who thought to record the event but never quite managed to. One day it was too late, the diesel had usurped steam on these expresses.
Jack Teasdale/T. J. Ermel Collection

Below left: Although apparently an up express, this was in fact an authorised headlamp code for station pilot engines. One of the once numerous Class J72s, No 68728 goes about its relatively mundane duties around the station in 1960. An NER design, the 'J72' was so successful that construction went on at various times between 1898 to 1951 with little alteration needed. This example was turned out new in 1922 from the nearby works of Armstrong Whitworth & Co. ***Jack Teasdale/ T. J. Ermel Collection***

Above: The excellent vista afforded from the old keep was well patronised by railway observers, as it is still today. In this mid-1950s view, looking towards Manors station, a 'V3' tank engine, No 67652, is awaiting orders to remove an empty carriage set to Heaton, whilst the empty coaches for the next Liverpool departure arrive from Heaton hauled by Class D20 No 62360. No 62360 would then wait in the west end bay platforms until it was time to depart with an afternoon Alnwick semi-fast, completing its diagram with the return working to Newcastle and the empty set put to bed at Heaton. Most of the property seen on the horizon made way for the mid-1960s developments during the T. Dan Smith era when the city skyline changed completely. ***Bob Payne***

Left: Dunston station, currently on the only route to the west, has had mixed fortunes, having being shut and reopened twice. Looking towards Norwood overhead signalbox at the junction with Norwood Yard and the staiths at Dunston, this photograph depicts it during a closed spell in 1955. Its current opening date was 1982 but today it sees few stopping trains and must surely be facing another closure. ***A. J. Wickens***

Above: Several steam locos are to be seen in this 1956 view from the northern end of Gateshead station. Approaching is one of the small group of Class O4 2-8-0s brought into Tyne Dock to help haul heavy traffic to and from Consett. On this occasion, however, No 63712 has only a 'light' coal load. The High Level Bridge today has two tracks together and a stringent speed/weight restriction as time begins to tell upon Robert Stephenson's 1847 masterpiece. ***J. W. Armstrong Trust Collection***

Above: An example of the Eastleigh-built EMUs which replaced the then aging NER examples, seen at Pelaw station in the winter of 1957. ***Bob Payne***

Below: Class K3 , No 61854, of Tweedmouth shed, restarts the afternoon Newcastle-Berwick stopping train at Morpeth on a rainy July day in 1960. ***Peter J. Robinson***

Above: The convergence, albeit at different heights, of the coastal route with the ECML at Benton led many photographers over the years to attempt this passing shot. Apart from Ian S. Carr, John Armstrong was the only other person known to accomplish it satisfactorily. Here is the evidence, achieved in the summer of 1956. An eastbound MetCam electric meets an up east coast express behind Class A1 No 60132 *Marmion*. ***J. W. Armstrong Trust Collection***

Above: Built by Kitson's in 1883 to a Stephenson long-boiler design was this tank locomotive, still hard at work in 1960 when photographed by Alan Thompson. This is the Swalwell area at the foot of the Derwent Valley; the engine is making its way up to Derwenthaugh coking plant. ***A. R. Thompson***

5 The Final Years of Steam (1963-1967)

Steam in the northeast died in the mid-1960s in common with the rest of BR, though this was one of the areas where heavy freight use survived longest and some surprising pre-Grouping survivors were to be found almost to the end.

Before looking at the final curtain-call of steam around Newcastle, let us first taste briefly the recipe upon which the excellence of northeastern locomotive engineering was founded and recall also some of the lesser achievements.

Gateshead, the centre of NER locomotive technology, enjoyed the reigns of three great chief mechanical engineers who together were in control for 60 years of the NER's 68-year life. They were Edward Fletcher (1854-83), Wilson Worsdell (1890-1910) and Sir Vincent Raven (1910-22). Their influence was unmistakable, as was the continuity of thinking, which showed in the clean and simple yet impressive lines of NER engines.

Gateshead Works also produced a draughtsman of world class in Walter Smith. He directed operations for more than 20 years. Robust freight engines were Smith's priority and two types lasted to not only serve the NER and the LNER but also to see almost 20 years' service in BR days. These were of course the 'T2' (later 'Q6') and 'P3' (later 'J27') mineral engines. The 'T2' in particular had roots in the first 'T' type brought in by Worsdell as far back as 1901. The resultant 120 'T2s' have even been described by historians of the past as the engines that 'won two wars' in this corner of England — there is no doubting their contribution and it would be an interesting exercise to calculate total mileage and tonnage

Below: The last survivor of the once numerous 'Q6' class of engines that dominated rail activity in the northeast is seen during one of its final labours for British Railways. The scrapyard beckoned soon after this August 1967 day, when No 63395 was photographed returning empty coal wagons from Stella South, Blaydon, to the pits in the Murton complex. No 63395 thwarted the cutters torch and was purchased by a Newcastle group of enthusiasts, intent upon preserving an example of these unsung heroes of two world wars for future generations to experience. ***A. R. Thompson***

moved by the class, both in the war years and total life service.

Between Fletcher and Worsdell there was a brief hiatus when matters were in the hands of a committee. The 'Tennant' series date from then. In 1888 Tennant locos put up fine performances on the East Coast route's 'Races to the North', repeating their efforts in 1895.

Sir Vincent Raven had a profound influence upon the years from 1896 up to World War 1. He was very much involved in the electrification of the Newcastle coastal lines in 1904. His ultimate aim was complete electrification of the East Coast main line — again, a war interrupted progress and another 74 years passed before it was achieved. So steam traction continued but even so records still tumbled; in 1914 the NER declared that the 12.20 Newcastle-Sheffield was the fastest-timed train in the British Empire — a riband which the East Coast route has seldom relinquished since (with due apologies to the Great Western!).

In 1905 the first 'autocars' (steam engine and coach in one unit) came into service at Hartlepool. They were introduced by the NER as an economy measure, in an attempt to hold down marginal passenger receipts where the motorbus and tram threat was cranking up. Inevitably this has been an uphill struggle for the railways ever since the mechanisation of road transport began and only now is the balance of public opinion shifting as realisation grows of the effects of exhaust emissions from fossil fuels (including coal burning of course!). At last, with electrification projects, including Tyneside Metro and the East Coast main line as two extremes, are railways claiming the environmental edge — though the fuel still has to be burned somewhere.

Another aspect of the NER's battle to win and keep passengers was its ticketing innovations. In 1896 it introduced 'zonal tickets' at fixed prices to traders, and to the general public it sold 1,000-mile tickets, which could be exchanged for individual tickets to any station on the line of route.

These great days had long passed by the mid-1950s, and there were fewer locomotives needed and fewer motive power depots to find them in — although it could be argued that the variety to be seen was as great as ever, if not greater. In the mid-1950s and into the rundown of steam, this was the pattern of Tyneside steam sheds.

In the immediate Newcastle city area were three locomotive depots, of which the main one was Gateshead — in spitting distance over the Tyne Gorge and supplier of main passenger power. To the east, and in a very much less cramped location, was Heaton Depot. Heaton supplied the next level of passenger services with power and naturally was well fixed to power the Newcastle-originating services, as in 90% of cases the empty coaches would be brought in from the sidings behind the shed. Heaton would supply power for many fast goods trains starting in the area and would repower much of the long distance East Coast goods that would lie-over outside the depot on the freight loops adjacent to the main line.

Third, and conspicuously close to Gateshead, was Borough Gardens — just around High Street curve on the Sunderland route and

Left: The 1960s scrapping programme saw massive inroads into the ranks of steam engines everywhere. Also fast disappearing were the many freight-only branch lines around the region. In 1963 enthusiasts organised a special train to tour every possible branch, knowing this may be the last opportunity for many locations. Here we see the special train passing Manors (North) station towards Jesmond and South Gosforth where it would eventually peel off to the left for Ponteland and thence into the heart of Northumberland and its many mineral railways.
A. R. Thompson

Right: A 1938 Met-Cam EMU traverses below the Cramlington Waggonway at Backworth on the outward journey to the coastal stations via Jesmond in summer 1966. There is no longer a station of this name on the replacement Metro route. The nearest station today is Palmersville. ***Author***

tucked away among many heavy engineering factories that hugged the Gateshead bank of the Tyne to the east. Borough Gardens gave power to the South Tyne-based slow / medium speed goods workings, a host of 'trippers' around the mineral or goods yards on both sides of the Tyne and shared shunting engine supply with Gateshead to relieve the latter's overcrowding. It was from here that the seemingly endless stream of 0-6-0s emerged to beaver away throughout the murkier parts of Tyneside.

This gives a very broad-brush description of work allocation, but the local enginemen's 'LDC' agreements went into much detail as to how the service supply responsibilities were distributed to these depots. It is not incorrect to say that the allocation was made on the basis of: first, the starting point of the traffic to be conveyed; second, the speed associated with this traffic (very often dependent on the train description in the Working timetable); and finally, the route to be taken from Newcastle — and thus dependent upon that depot's men knowing the route and loco characteristics to be deployed. To complicate matters however, each depot had 'inherited factors', often of obscure origins but which were difficult to break down and had been fought for by the LDC representatives in order to secure not only importance for the depot but (and very important) to increase earning power! These agreements were often hard-driven and made after several days locked in what seemed like a kipper curing shed. They were very jealously guarded!

Within the 'outer radius' of depots serving the city lay Blaydon Depot along the Newcastle & Carlisle route to the west, and the famous Scotswood Road.

Traditionally the power supplier to the lines radiating to the west, on which it stood, Blaydon was much involved in a mix of fast goods (Classes K1 & B1) and mineral transport up the steeply graded valleys north and south (Classes J39 & Q6) with a sprinkling of 'locals' that invariably moved behind whatever was too weak for heavy work — often a 'J21'. Blaydon's engines roamed far and wide and it was a widely held belief in the area that whatever and wherever a wartime load was destined, then if all else failed a Blaydon man would know the route! It is recorded that Blaydon men had worked throughout (with their engines) to Sheffield and Manchester to the south and to Glasgow to the north, with one individual boasting of having worked a 63-hour continuous shift (Stranraer and back on a Class 8 goods, perhaps).

These four depots were the main arterial suppliers to the many traffic flows that criss-crossed through the Newcastle area in the final great days of steam in the district. The illustrations recall typical scenes over the years.

Finally (and it would be ungrateful not to honour the much acclaimed work of Aiden Fuller, the author) an extract from the Loco Shed Directory, one of the abc titles published by Ian Allan, which was de rigueur when going on a distant 'shed bash', will remind many people of how they first became familiar with the three main Newcastle area sheds. The words may also bring back memories of first skirmishes with irate running foremen, many of whom must have confiscated quite a few of those little books in their time!

Left: Already referred to in a previous picture, the 1963 North Eastern Tour took i many lines that were barely surviving. This leg started at South Shields and came up th Stanhope & Tyne road behind the powerful Class Q7 survivor, No 63460. At this stage of the journey from Consett, 'K1' No 62027 has the honour of leading the wa out towards an even more remote location — Waskerley (a place associated with the first stirrings of the industrial revolution in these parts as it was also linked with the Stockton & Darlington Railway). The tour i seen passing through Rowley station, itself now known as having been rebuilt brick by brick at Beamish Museum.
Beamish Museum

52A GATESHEAD
The shed is on the north side of the line west of Gateshead West station. The yard is visible from the line.

From Gateshead East station
Turn left outside Gateshead East station and almost immediately right into Half Moon Lane. Continue under a low railway bridge and ascend a short flight of steps on the left-hand side, immediately under the bridge. A paved path leads from the top of these steps past the rear of Gateshead West station and bears right past the loco works to the shed. Walking time five minutes.

From Gateshead West station.
Turn right outside Gateshead West station into a narrow street and bear right almost immediately into Half Moon Lane. Follow directions as from Gateshead East station.

52B HEATON
The shed is in the fork of the main and North Shields lines east of the station. The yard is partially visible from both lines.

Turn left outside the south side of Heaton station along North View. Continue along this road to the end. A path leads to the shed from a gate in Chillingham Road opposite the end of North View. Walking time 5 minutes.

Note— There are conductor rails in the vicinity of the coal stage.

52C BLAYDON
The shed is on the south side of the Newcastle line east of the station. The yard is partially visible from the line.

Turn left outside Blaydon station along Tyne Street and continue over the level crossing alon the main road to Newcastle (A695) parallel to the railway. The shed entrance is on the left-hand side. Walking time 10 minutes. United bu services operate from a bus station close to Newcastle station past the shed entrance.

Left: Class V2 No 60913, of Gateshead, stands at the head of the 4.30pm 'stopper' to Berwick-on-Tweed at Central station in November 1963. In the background a DMU awaits departure time with a local South Shields train.
A. R. Thompson

Left: A 1964 view of the Scotswood area with Delaval Sidings located to the west of the city. To the right are coal cells above the Scotswood Road and signs of the immense industrial muscle that was Armstrong's works spread along the right, fringing the Tyne. Heading back to the collieries with empty 16-ton mineral wagons is yet another Class J27.
M. Dunnett

Left: Newcastle west end pilot engine in this August 1963 picture is one of the two 'J72s' that were repainted in NER apple green at the behest of the Railway Correspondence & Travel Society. No 68736, with a York (50A) shedplate, potters in Platform 12. Behind are vans in the short parcels docks and the spire of All Saints towers above.
Dave Smith

Left: The station pilot was normally Gateshead's own No 68723, also in the apple green livery of the old NER. Prominent in the background is the Forth Banks headquarters of the Engineer's Department. spring 1963. ***Dave Smith***

Above: Empty stock for York pulls up for water over on the goods line and the fireman sees to things at the back end of a 'V2' that looks in very smart external condition. August 1963.
Dave Smith

Left: A fireman's view of this famous vista to the north, looking directly at the castle keep from which Newcastle's name is derived. Occasional failures during the steam-diesel transition years of the 1960s led to unexpected last minute diesel replacements by any engine fit enough to work. On this occasion it seems that the diesel on this Liverpool-Newcastle express expired at Leeds and ex-LMS Class 5 No 44864 has had the unexpected pleasure of express haulage in its twilight period. It is 28 August 1965.
T. J. Ermel

Right: All said and done, there was never anything quite like an 'A4' to bring out the boys in grown men! Five years after being saved from scrapping No 4498 *Sir Nigel Gresley* takes centre stage yet again in Newcastle's west end bay platform and mimics a night express of a bygone era. It is 1972 and the diesel unit in the adjacent platform kindly points out the classification of the visitor. ***T. J. Ermel***

Below right: On south Tyneside, railway activities centred on Tyne Dock locomotive depot, a shed that had grown over the years in tune with the increased shipping facilities afforded by the NER. It grew in a hotchpotch manner from 1861, and by this 1965 view was struggling to keep its 30 or so engines in good running order, as it sank under general neglect and weariness. Glimpsed in the middle of this view, between two ex-NER 'Q6s', is a BR-built '9F', representing the ultimate steam power on BR. No 92097 is being coaxed into life with fire irons in preparation for a turn of duty lifting 500 tons of imported ore over the old Stanhope & Tyne mineral route to Consett. The last steam-hauled ore train ran on 19 November 1966; thereafter Type 2 diesels in multiple worked up the bank. The closure of the Iron & Steel Works ultimately came in 1982. ***Author***

Left: Steam engines pass at Castle Keep Junction in the autumn of 1965. 'A1' No 60134 *Foxhunter* had deputised for a failed diesel in the Leeds area on the 13.05 Liverpool-Newcastle and made a welcome sight at this late stage to add variety to an otherwise predictable passenger power portfolio. Held just beyond the diamond crossing is 'Q6' No 63381, which had just been released after repairs at Heaton and had found a staged load of coal for Stella power station. This is thought to be No 60134's last visit to Tyneside. ***Peter J. Robinson***

6
Tyneside Freight

In 1913 the NER's *Trade & Commerce Digest* described Newcastle in these terms:

'Newcastle has a population of 274,955 and is the commercial centre of the northern counties. It was created a city in 1882. Within the city boundaries are the Elswick works of Messrs Armstrong, Whitworth & Co where battleships were built and armed prior to the establishment of the firm's great naval yards at Walker, and the locomotive & marine engineering works of Messrs Hawthorn, Leslie & Co. It is interesting to recall that George Stephenson, in the year 1824, founded in South Street, Newcastle, the first factory for the production of locomotive engines.

'Flour milling and the manufacture of chemicals are also important industries. The extent of the manufactures, however, gives little idea of the immense business controlled from Newcastle, as many shipowners and colliery companies have their headquarters in the city though the bulk of their transactions are carried on elsewhere.

'There is a large sheep and cattle market, and upwards of 15,000 wagons of livestock are despatched annually from Newcastle Forth Goods station, which is the largest forwarding point for the traffic on the North Eastern system. The other principal rail forwardings from Newcastle stations are flour (50,000), grain (45,000) and iron/steel (25,000 tons).'

Consett is referred to thus:

'Consett, with a population of 12,151, is situated 12 miles south-west of Newcastle. The ironworks, which are 900 feet above sea level, contain eight blast furnaces and consume 550,000 tons of iron ore yearly. The works have an annual output of a quarter of a million tons of iron and steel, the whole of which, both in and out, passes over the North Eastern Railway.'

The area was well supplied with goods facilities and was indisputably the biggest earner in this corner of England. If we look first to the immediate city radius of, say, three miles, then we find half a dozen very large installations for just this business.

The closest to Central station was the Forth Goods Depot. This accommodated cattle, timber, beer and general commodities that were slightly less vulnerable than, say, city food supply requirements of a 'use next day' description, which tended to be routed into the New Bridge Street Goods Depot across town.

Forth Goods employed in excess of 500 people at its height, post-1950, when it was

Above: On a parallel route to the Avenue branch was the busy Blyth & Tyne mineral railway. It acted as the coal artery from the pit heartland of Northumberland to the staiths below Percy Main. Not initially blessed with the easiest operational conditions, poor steam maintenance by the mid-1960s made this haulage more difficult. By the summer of 1966 the motive power authorities were desperate for additional locomotive cover for the now-failing NER examples which had been flogged almost to a standstill. Help came with the offer of now redundant ex-LMR locomotives in the shape of Ivatt '4MTs'. It is evident that their design did not have mineral haulage up 1 in 50 gradients in mind as can be seen in this view of 18 July 1966. Recently transferred, No 43101 has ground to a halt on Earsdon Bank (near Backworth) and after a 20min pause has to thank Class K1 No 62057 (passing with a brake van) for a push to the top at Blue Bell crossing. ***Author***

Right: Forth goods depot. With the best part of 200 wagons visible in this view of the complex. Taken in conditions considered grey even by 1930's standards, nothing can detract from the evidence of the backbreaking and repetitive labours that must have been the lot for so many men who passed through the gates here throughout its 100 years. The camera is looking down onto the area known as Victoria Goods, which had road access from the romantically named Shot Factory Lane. This access enabled farmers' and brewers' carts to park alongside wagons. The hive of activity includes unloading wagons of timber, sheeting-up for transit and a flock of sheep being driven, perhaps to the nearby abattoirs or market. Today, Newcastle Arena sits squarely in the middle of this prospect no trace of these sidings remain. ***J. W. Armstrong Trust Collection***

operating around the clock, invariably for seven days per week. Staff worked long 10hr shifts, with few breaks and plenty of overtime if they had any reserves left! Understandably the labour turnover was high and there seemed always to be adverts locally for people prepared to train as checkers and porters. The Forth owed its fine position relative to city deliveries to the Newcastle & Carlisle Railway's foresight in buying up this huge tract of land to the east of Scotswood (feeling sure that was the direction the main line would go and so aiming to make a killing!). It could be argued that the only obstacle to it becoming the perfect goods location was its height above the river and the logistics of getting goods up quickly and without repeated handling. This factor guaranteed the prolonged life of the New Bridge Street Depot — even after a highly successful bombing raid destroyed 60% of it — and its associated Trafalgar Yard goods facility.

New Bridge Street, built upon land originally chosen as the Blyth & Tyne terminus for the city, was within city limits. Its goods could be trucked to city shops within an hour of arrival, although to get to this stage might involve several trips from the main yards, due to the

minor aspect of its source point, Trafalgar Goods Yard. However, it held the ace for import and export speed, with quick access to the Tyne's Scandinavian Wharves via the half-mile semi-circular tunnel. It was this link that kept the depot operating in a semi-derelict condition from the time of the bombing through to the late 1960s when the shipping trade was lost by BR.

A little further along to the east, Heaton boasted a great assortment of goods handling equipment but was mainly involved directly with road deliveries in connection with some coal cells in the north yard. It had access almost straight from Heaton steam shed into companies such as Metal Box and Parsons, who had private sidings running straight in.

Gateshead boasted several and various minor goods facilities before the emergence of TCFD and Tyne Marshalling Yard in the early 1960s effectively wiped them all from the map overnight. Briefly, facilities south of the river included: Blaydon Goods, Gateshead Town Goods, Gateshead Park Lane (which became the site of TCFD Goods Depot), Redheugh Goods, together with small handling facilities at many stations.

Above: The construction of the 80-acre trading estate in the Team Valley at Gateshead in the early 1930s opened up countless opportunities for the LNER but by the 1960s only three traders were actively passing goods to BR. Of the fruit and vegetable market, British Road Services and Durham Steel only the first mentioned was consistently keeping the local tripper from Tyne Yard active. On this occasion the 1956-built diesel-mechanical pilot engine brings in French and Spanish produce towards the dedicated undercover framework of the unloading bay ahead near the north end of the estate. ***Author***

Left: Interior view, Forth goods depot. Town deliveries of smaller items were undertaken by rulleymen with their carts and horses. Each cart, with the legend LNER written out fully along its waist, stands under a numbered dock, each representing a different district for delivery. Loading and dispatch was a complex, slow and often long process, lightened only by the bond that existed between man and horse (the latter to be replaced by the Scammell). Today the roofless ruin of the site is partly used by the Eastern Infrastructure Maintenance Unit to store materials and on-track machinery. ***Courtesy Newcastle City Libraries***

Left: At one time, overlooking Park Lane goods and Borough Gardens loco shed, was this large goods warehouse known as Gateshead Eldon Street goods. This 1966 view shows the final days for Eldon Street, as it was removed completely the following year when the destination of this load on the Sunderland goods line, Tyneside Central Freight Depot, came into full use. TCFD (as it was known) was opened by Dr Beeching on 15 October 1963. As its name suggests, it meant the demise of 10 older depots. TCFD, it was boasted in the publicity, 'serves 700 square miles of Northumberland and Durham, including all industrial Tyneside. Each week it deals with 400-500 wagon loads of "smalls" and up to 200 wagons of full-load with transit times subsequently reduced.' In practice, these numbers never materialised and TCFD contracted gradually until in the 1980s it became a depot shared with other businesses in a last-ditch attempt to pay its way. Closed by 1987 and demolished by 1995, the land now stands idle awaiting its next chapter. ***M. Dunnett***

Left: The staple diet of the NER/LNER throughout to the NE region of BR was the export of coal principally from the Tyne. Although Hull and the Wear made huge contributions to revenue in this respect, it was the tonnage exported from the Tyne over the years that became the main component of railway expansion. Exporting of minerals from the Tyne became well organised by the 17th century, but the big changes came around the 1890s when the river was improved to enable navigation above the bridges. The NER's dedicated coal staiths that sprung up in consequence in 1893, such as these at Dunston, Gateshead, allowed speedy dispatch of steam colliers and really opened up the trade to foreign interests. ***Author***

Left: A glimpse into the old style world of Gateshead Eldon Street. Some product names have since vanished but cornflakes were obviously popular then, while Capstan did take the strain here, as capstans performed the work of pilot engines to move wagons slowly up and down the positions.
British Railways Board

Centre left: In and around the heavy industries connected with the river between Newcastle and Walker a supply of 'J72' engines was made available, mainly from Heaton. In this mid-1950s view, No 68713 is gainfully employed at the eastern extremity of the quayside rail network near Glasshouse Bridge, while corporation crane No 5 lifts metal sheets from plate wagons.
A. R. Thompson Collection

Below left: The region was dotted with exchange sidings where British Rail and NCB exchanged traffic. These were the hand-over places. British Rail crews would drop off a rake of waggons and depart; some time afterwards (sometimes many hours), an NCB shunt engine would appear and lead the rake under the discharge plant and replace the load where it was found by BR, and so on, day and night. This work was co-ordinated by the Mineral Leading Controllers at Newcastle Central offices. It was a job in which you had to keep your nerve! This example of exchange sidings is at Jarrow, Pontop Junction. BR loads are seen at the left awaiting 'J27s' or 'Q6s' to lead them out. NCB internal loads are to the right whilst ahead are Jarrow, NCB staiths and the cranes of the shipbuilding industry, 1960.
Colin Mountford

Left: At the other end of the Quay Tunnel, at Trafalgar Yard, electric No 26501 changes to overhead power and emerges into daylight with what looks like a railway sleeper load. The tunnel was half a mile long and had both entrances facing the same direction — west. Add to this 180° curve a ruling gradient of 1 in 28 and it can be appreciated that steam traction was going to have all sorts of problems. Worked by steam from 1870 to 1905, the advent of electricity was an answer to a complex problem and the tunnel became third-rail powered. It is 1954 and Heaton's only 'J77' (at that time) hovers around for transfer traffic. Wires are everywhere and even above, in New Bridge Street, trolleybus wires predominate. Although both trolleys and 'ES1s' have now gone, overhead wires have not, thanks to the adjacent ECML route.
J. W. Armstrong Trust Collection

Centre left: At the Percy Main end of the Blyth & Tyne were numerous differently-shaped staith structures that all went to make up Northumberland Dock — second only to Tyne Dock for its coal export figures. Almost every private coal company had a staith here, although as costs snowballed rationalisation and sharing of resources was eventually forced on them. A resemblance to early American structures can be excused, as these structures are more likely to have provided the model for those in the US. ***E. Brack***

Below left: On Heaton shed's penultimate day of full depot activities, 15 June 1963, 204hp diesel shunter D2311 hauls in 'ES1' electric No 26500 for the final time, pending a move to South Gosforth. Although the 'ES1' could have transported itself via third-rail to Heaton, its steam 'mate' from Trafalgar Yard did the hauling and was the order of things up until then. Electric working of the quayside branch ceased shortly after this date. No 26500 then went through a turbulent period of 'on-off' preservation. First moved into storage at Hellifield and later Rugby, it finally appeared at Leicester's Stonygate Museum until closure in 1975. Its last move was into the NRM at York, where it is now painted in NER colours and not how most of us remember it! ***Ian S. Carr***

Right: Norwood coke works situated at the northern end of the Team valley in Gateshead linked with the British Rail system via the Blaydon-Newcastle route. It is well remembered by local people for its pungent sulphuric product and had a variety of small tank engines that buzzed about day and night. The site was cleared during 1988-9 for the National Garden Festival in 1990. Today it is partly landscaped, partly built on; not a trace exists of the works — above the ground! ***A. R. Thompson***

Left: The business side of the Norwood/Dunston complex was the older outer staith (the newer inner basin staith having been fired and weakened in the 1950s). Dating from 1894, the staith structure formed the centrepiece of the Gateshead National Garden Festival in 1990 and survives today as an example of a complex, all-timber structure that has endured many scares following numerous shipping prangs. In this 1960 view taken from the river, *Bahia be Palma* is being teemed into its aft hold. Just visible above the vessel's bridge is a diminutive 204hp shunter. The towers seen beyond belong to Redheugh gasworks.***John Johnson/ Author's collection***

Left: British Railways and Tyne Improvement Committee worked in unison within the confines of Albert Edward Dock. On this particular day, 27 July 1955, the dock pilot No 68283 shunts a mixed rake of waggons that also includes TIC No 27. ***D. G. Charlton***

Left: A most historic part in the shaping of not only Gateshead's evolution but all Tyneside's, was the Greenesfield incline/Redheugh Bank Foot area, seen in its final railway shape in 1978. Not only does this location give a commanding view of the bridges but it was the end-on junction of the early Brandling Railway with the Newcastle & Carlisle. Through the second arch, far right, of the King Edward Bridge was the route taken by transfer traffic, down a steep incline from Greenesfield. Early pictures show titanic struggles to lift traffic from Tyne level up here and sometimes two or even three locos were used to push up a mere five or six vehicles. Below, and running alongside at river level, was the route to Redheugh station — the first terminus of the Newcastle & Carlisle Railway. It can be seen that by 1978 this was predominantly wasteland awaiting a post-industrial revival. ***Author***

Left: Scotswood Junction, the point where the two routes to Carlisle split into north or south of the Tyne, eventually re-uniting just before Prudhoe. About to travel the North Tyne route at this rarely photographed location is 'Q6' No 63409 with a coal load for Stella North power station in 1965. Today the trackbed forms a dedicated cycle path to Ovingham. ***Peter J. Robinson***

Below left: Incoming 'K1s' ousted several world-weary NER specimens from 1965 onwards on mineral work. This one, No 62027, has taken a particularly tortuous route with its coal load from a Northumberland pit and appears to have been prevented from making a direct approach by Sunday engineering work. It is about to join the ECML at Heaton Junction after leading coal along the Blyth & Tyne via Percy Main and Walkergate. The location is now the platform area of the Metro station Chillingham Road. Heaton steam shed was replaced by the redesigned HST servicing depot in the 1970s and is now simply an area of sidings. ***Author***

Right: When Tyne Marshalling Yard was constructed on a green-field site at Lamesley it swallowed up the work of 15 smaller sidings that had operated from NER days. On 21 December 1964 'Q6 No 63368 is about to attack the gradient onto the flyover to gain access to reception sidings. ***M. Dunnett***

Below right: Tyne Marshalling Yard, situated three miles south of Newcastle at Lamesley, grew out of the British Railways modernisation programme started in 1955 to breath fresh life into the war-worn railways. It was opened by Lord Hailsham in 1963, this view shows the city of Newcastle on the far horizon and below is the control tower that incorporated a signalbox and two very large relay rooms. The fans of sidings radiating down from the hump top and the path taken by wagons through the two banks of retarders is evident. The East Coast route skirts the yard to the right although the down slow line went the long way around the yard fringe to the left. At the north end can be seen the small loco depot and the office block.

Humping of wagons ceased in 1983 and once or twice radical remodelling was proposed; however, with the freight revival under EWS, the yard is once again buzzing and people are returning to work here. ***Author***

Left: Mention of Tyneside cannot forgo a brief glimpse of Consett Iron & Steel Works, the main raison d'être for Tyne Dock Shed and the only route that gave Northerners a glimpse of one of Riddles's massive 2-10-0 '9F' engines hard at work. In this instance, in August 1964, No 92064 has just discharged almost 500 tons of Peruvian ore down onto the belts on the roof of County Durham.
Peter J. Robinson

Above: Of interest because few parcel trains in the northeast originated outside of Newcastle, was this service, the 16.00 Brian Mills service (Sunderland) to King's Cross York Way. In September 1965 two-tone green D1520 on this service meets ex-works 'J27' No 65814 at Ryhope Grange. The two types are some six generations apart in technological terms — quite a contrast. ***Peter J. Robinson***

Below: South of Percy Main, the Blyth & Tyne relinquished control of operations to the Tyne Improvement Commission for the journey down into 'staiths land'. As can be seen from old maps of this area, there were many routes and options, and a steady unrelenting build-up of fine coal on point blades would give TIC staff endless problems. At No 5 Signalbox junction on 24 September 1958, a rake of 5 21-ton hoppers have agreed to differ concerning the intended route of their 'J27'. The rest of the load has disappeared towards Low Row, thence Coble Dene. A colourful and somewhat acrimonious dispute ensues regarding the cause, while TIC track men probe for evidence! There was never a dull moment in these parts. ***J. W. Armstrong Trust Collection***

7
Newcastle Central

As some old Inn for active life once stood
Where cross-roads met upon the great highways,
The railway station, to adventurers good,
Is the great turn-pike of these later days;
Here we meet, part, welcome, or say goodbye,
A little changing crowd beneath the changeless sky.

Acknowledgement to Chapman & Hall Ltd for part of 'The Railway Station' by E. M. Martin, from 'Apollo to Christ'.

Alan Wells writes in The Blyth & Tyne Branch Parts 1-3:

'We look to our main line station at Newcastle today and enterprisingly see marketing partnerships between train operators and other businesses, using not only the refound concourse area but shop fronts where once only imperious Victorian officialdom shouted out; but hang on, wasn't this area cluttered with marketing furniture once before, in another time?

'The passenger of an earlier age would have had quite a fight to get to the train. He would have to successfully manipulate himself past the machines of Nestlé's (then pronounced Nesils) penny bars of chocolate, and those of Fry's, at one time displaying the much loved Five-Boys motif.

'The next hazard was the Beech Nut Chewing Gum machine (which when the arrow pointed to you gave you an extra). While keeping an eye on the chocolate and the gum you would almost certainly trip over the zealously obstructive weighing

Below: Commanding excellent vision across the large framework of steel comprising the Newcastle Diamond Crossing was the not inconsiderable Newcastle No 1 signalbox with its 'flying wings'. In this 1949 view, from the end of old Platform No 8, engine No 67687 brings in a Middlesbrough train of a (even then) vintage stock consist, whilst Class J72 No 68723 potters past displaying its new British Railways look; (14 years later, No 68723 could be seen in NER apple green.) Of special interest here is the 'caller' who can be seen in his lair. The reason for his deployment here reflects the fact that without the eyes of today's track-circuits, a signalman in this position and with many traffic movements, could quite easily give the wrong route and virtually bring the station to a halt. This 'caller' therefore acted as an extra pair of eyes for the signalman and, when the fog dropped, would also shout down to crews to confirm they were who they were thought to be. Unsophisticated, but functionally necessary. ***J. W. Armstrong Trust Collection***

Left: An ever-present on empty coach work up until 1963 was Class V3 No 67654. Here it looks well turned out — perhaps a result of a recent visit to the works.
J. W. Armstrong Trust Collection

machine platform and, having got back to your feet, you might be attracted over to the perfume dispensers (they had but a brief reign — perhaps Eau de Cologne was an unhappy bed partner with "Water o' Tyne"?).

'Having thought you were now safe to board the 3.40pm slow to Brockley Whins, a large post box, only cut down a bit shorter, square in shape and very pregnant, resting on four splay-foot legs, would entice you into printing out the name of your favourite Newcastle footballer of the day. The printing process was tedious and if you became greedy to get extra letters (over the allotted 18) then the name-punch would begin to over-punch letters, so that the last letter would have them all beaten onto the metal strip like alphabet soup gone crazy. There should have been a warning accompanying the machine to tell which LNER Directors (also adorning boiler sides!) could be beaten out in metal...you were definitely pushing your luck with *Sir Ralph Wedgewood*.'

As Joyce reflects, on the 1930s in particular, in Roads and Rails of Tyne & Wear (1900-1980):

'There [was] a lighter side to it all. Forget for a moment the years of depression... the waiting for a tramcar (or trolley) in the wet street and the cold ride on the wooden seated open top deck. Instead recall the sunny ride through Gosforth Park or beside the sea at Whitley Bay or Roker... recollect youthful enchantment in the great cavern of Newcastle Central when it pulsated to big green steam locomotives and sleek red and white electric trains.'

Joyce concludes by advising the reader to take a look again at Tyne and Wear transport of yesterday, as it is 'instructive in reminding us how the present has grown out of the past'.

'For so much of the time that railways were developing let us remember that the area would be plunged into uncertainties and it was often reflected in revenue. Balanced against the many minus points was an occasional plus for Central station receipts, when the "Magpies" were playing well and a long cup run guaranteed many lucrative additionals. It was no secret that many local railway officials would be seen on Saturdays inside the turnstile cubicles or even stewarding people into the ground. Newcastle Central and St James' Park were inextricably linked in the people-moving business!'

With the closure of Heaton Depot in 1963, Gateshead was left to bear the brunt of locomotive maintenance work for the area, although Heaton went on working with a small number of fitters into 1966 and continued to act as an overflow dump for stored locomotives awaiting disposal and the occasional work on specials. 1963 also saw the mechanisation of freight handling, with both Tyne Yard and Gateshead's new freight depot being officially opened by Ernest Marples, then Minister of Transport and the man forever remembered for his appointment of Dr Beeching as Chairman of the BR Board.

The changeover from steam to diesel on express workings through Newcastle was all but completed by this year, making Brian Perren's comments of less than four years earlier seem hopelessly out of date — such was the speed with which the diesel changeover occurred. Rural tentacles reaching out from Tyneside, such as the North and South Tyne Valley branches to Redesmouth and Allendale, had ceased to be passenger destinations in the 1950s and now in the 1960s lost their freight trippers too, and closing completely.

The 1970s saw little spectacular change in and around the area, with DMUs a sluggish and unappetising replacement for the nifty, swaying Met-Cam electrics of a previous era. Local service receipts slid down as train and station investment also plummeted. A rise in vandalism was a feature that has continued ever since, and most local rail travellers gladly put up with the discomforts of the great 'Metro' dig-in that finally saw action after years of squabbling between BR and local transport councillors concerning the way forward for Tyneside.

Metro and bus interchangeability from 1983 made Tyneside the envy of European metropolises, themselves searching to find the long-term and cost-effective answer to car strangulation. Tyneside, with one of the lowest car ownership ratios in the country, was an ideal location to prove the worth of 'Metro'. It was a short-lived honeymoon for the commuter though, as the 1980s ended in disarray, with bus deregulation ending the happy-hour that had actually witnessed a drift back to public transport in increasing numbers — a sad and retrograde step.

The mid-1980s witnessed the age profile of the majority of the diesel fleet passing over the proverbial yard-arm and even later types, such as the Brush Class 47s were pushed into ad hoc work while others needed re-engining to eke out their existence. Enter the Class 60s for the remaining coal work and the disappearance of the once common and much admired Class 37s that had borne the brunt of pre-pit strike tonnages.

The 1990s brought profound and sweeping changes that finally cleared away the last few remnants associated with the gloom and dirt of a steam railway. The 1959 signalbox between platforms 9 and 10 (now 3 and 4) went, and in came a computer wonder control centre — over the river on BR property that once accommodated the railwaymen's laundry near Gateshead shed. The station underwent rigorous cosmetic surgery, receiving more than a mere face-lift; what it experienced resembled more a rebirth and was in line with the electric age to follow. The changes, developing further the work already undertaken in the mid-1980s on the concourse/travel centre area, completely opened up the vista, leaving no sign of the dirty black corners or cluttered areas of former times.

Old platform 10, with its unnecessary long curving profile, was at last straightened, thus ensuring that the new Mark 4 coaches would have no yawning gaps into which little or old feet might feel attracted. Terrazzo tiling was further extended and the roof support curves, still in 'tall-ship' timbers, suddenly shone out and proclaimed their gracefulness to all with a mind just to look up. Central was at last more like the dream envisaged by Dobson so long ago.

On a more global level, rationalisation of track everywhere ensured that there was no place to 'hide' spare sets — or anything else for that matter. The new Eastern IMU (Infrastructure Maintenance Unit) housed in the Forth offices undertook to keep what was left to run on in tip-top condition for the customer — the train operating companies.

Right: From an early batch of 'J72s', pilot No 68680 was once ever-present at this spot at the west end of Newcastle Central, being familiarly addressed by the hordes of spotters who congregated upon the nearby wall. Beyond is the black mass of the Forth Goods yard. The area upon which the engine stands, as far as the eye can see, is now a car park, nearby is now the new Telewest Arena (which was built on the wasteland that was once the Forth Goods sidings).
J. W. Armstrong Trust Collection

As we move towards the new century, Central continues to evolve into a retail centre. It is now actually pleasant to await a delayed train. Moving further ahead, the new vision of train operator Sea Containers for Central will undoubtedly result in an environment well placed to 'bat the breeze' and absorb the many displays within this cultural centre — the spiritual heart of Tyneside and a vibrant city — and definitely 'the one you have got to come back for!'

Right: Newcastle Platform 8 in this photograph is today Platform No 2 and mainly used in the northbound direction. In this 1954 view, Class A3 No 60086 *Gainsborough* prepares to return home at the head of the up 'Queen of Scots' Pullman. ***J. W. Armstrong Trust Collection***

Left: A view from just in front of No 3 Signalbox showing the sprawl of routes to either the Elswick direction or (right) over the King Edward Bridge for the south. The second starting signal gantry is aligned with the platform ends behind the larger all-routes gantry. This picture may have been arranged for a quiet Sunday morning if the leisurely nature of activities is anything to go by. ***Real Photographs***

Below right: The solidly constructed porte-cochère (or portico) of John Dobson is a startling statement of travel intent, although at this period of its history it shows signs of weather and environment malaise. Neville Street is a focal point for bus to bus, east to west, interchange. Today it also has the added ingredient of not only Metro transfers but connections with the Pacer train shuttle service that links the city to the big attraction of Gateshead Metro Centre. In this old view, trolleybus No 540 is on service 40. It was one of the 1948-50 builds to replace 1935 models. No 540 and its sisters were withdrawn in favour of more versatile motor buses on 1 October 1966 — a year prior to the end of the electric train service. The wheel has now almost turned full circle, with Metro and ECML trains now back on electricity. Could it be that Newcastle will follow the example of Manchester and Sheffield and reintroduce trams one day? ***J. W. Armstrong Trust Collection***

Right: It is 1959. Men in uniform are a common sight; it is de rigueur to carry a macintosh and the wearing of a trilby showed a certain status had been achieved — quite what, I've never been too sure! Midweek return travel to London is 49s (£2.45p!) and the Stationmaster was housed next door to the Bergen/Fred Olsen Lines shipping agents. A rush-hour queue has formed for platform 5 where the departure display (centrally in the background) still announces the 4.50pm departure, perhaps explaining some disgruntled looks. Another explanation may however be that the departure blind has to be manually wound up every so often! Orange and curved board notices announce facilities and not one space is wasted that can house a locker or dispensing machine. The seemingly ungoverned array of advertisements presents the public with a bewildering image and the hotchpotch style is so bad it is almost creative.
J. W. Armstrong Trust Collection

Above: This view, taken some yards further to the east of the previous view, records the late 1960s scene, by when DMUs have taken over the majority of semi-fast starters from these east bay platforms. The metal 'spiked' barriers that enclose the train area form not only a physical but also a psychological barrier to anyone even thinking of fare-dodging. Their association with prison bars reflects the military air of operations that pervaded until the open station concept had barriers crumbling everywhere from the mid-1970s onwards. The curved orange is replaced with corporate BR white (with the notable exception of the Centurion tearoom notices). Careful examination is repaid.
J. W. Armstrong Trust Collection

Appendices

Appendix 1

Sidings, Junctions, Collieries and Works listed in the Newcastle Area, 1956

Connected to Heaton Junction:
J. Arnott & Sons
Heaton Foundry Co Ltd
Heaton Junction (Public or common user)
Hunter's Coal Depot
Imperial Tobacco Co
Metal Box Co
Needler's Ltd
Newcastle Co-operative Society's Coal Depot
Nicholson's Chemical Works
Nicholson's Dope & Varnish
C. A. Parsons & Co Ltd, Heaton Works
F. Turnbull & Co

Connected to Newcastle Station:
Associated Lead Manufacturers Ltd
Forth Cattle Dock
Forth Hydraulic Engine House
Forth Provender Warehouse

Connected to New Bridge Street:
Carruther's Granary
Central Electricity Authority, Pandon Dene Siding
A. Guinness & Son Ltd Warehouse
J. Heinz & Co Warehouse
New Bridge Coal Sidings & Depots
Red Barns Manure Wharf
Schweppes Ltd Warehouse

Connected to Newcastle Quay:
Co-operative Society's Grain & General Warehouse
Newcastle Corporation Wharves Nos 3-26
Spillers Ltd, Tyne Mills

Connected to the Forth Goods:
English Steel Corporation Ltd, Elswick Works
Northern Gas Board, Elswick Works
Railway Street Coal & Lime Depots
Robt. Stephenson & Hawthorns Ltd
Vickers-Armstrong Ltd, Elswick Ordnance & Engineering Wks and Wharf

Connected with Elswick station:
E. J. Jobling Purser & Co
Tyne Grease & Oil Co

Appendix 2

Some facts about Central station

• In 1958 it handled 14,665,968 passengers.

• In 1871 the original building was enlarged by construction of an island platform on the south side (today's Platforms 3 and 4), bringing the total number of platforms to nine. A further enlargement took place in 1877, increasing the number to 12 platforms. The final development (before the 1990 changes) was in 1894 when the east end concourse was added to bring the final total up to 15 platforms, though only three through platforms existed.

• The Royal Station Hotel was added in 1894.

• North Tyneside electrics began running from the east end of the station in 1904. South Tyneside electrics began running, also from the east end, in 1938. Platforms 1-6 were at the east end and were equipped with third-rail, although most of the trains came and went from Platforms 1-3, with the South Tyne trains using Platform 6.

• Newcastle was often seriously disadvantaged by trains running out of 'path' (timetabled time). These would disrupt the quite fine 'time slots' on the through platforms. How many of us still today have experienced an excellent run — even early — until Newcastle, only to be told, 'we are awaiting a platform'?

• In addition to the three through platforms were four through goods lines on the south side outside the train shed.

• Completely new electric lighting, installed shortly after opening in 1850, made such a difference in winter that it was said many came to the station to enjoy a good, clear read in the sunshine! The lighting was completely updated in 1958.

• Colour-light signalling was introduced throughout in 1956-7 and on 12 April 1959 a new signalbox was commissioned on (old) platform 9 within the platform building. This replaced four boxes, Nos 1, 2, 3 and Manors.

Appendix 3

A brief summary of the main named trains, 1959.

From the South

Newcastle Arrival	Title
11.27	'North Briton'
12.46	'Morning Talisman'
13.59	'Elizabethan (pass-time)'
14.45	'Flying Scotsman'
18.11	'Heart of Midlothian'
20.30	'Afternoon Talisman'
21.32	'Tees-Tyne Pullman'
01.14	'Aberdonian'
04.46	'Night Scotsman'
06.31	'Tynesider'

To the South

Newcastle Departure	Title
01.22	'Night Scotsman'
02.22	'Aberdonian'
09.25	'Tees-Tyne Pullman'
10.49	'Morning Talisman'
11.52	'Elizabethan (pass-time)'
12.21	'Flying Scotsman'
15.56	'Heart of Midlothian'
17.00	*'The 5pm'
18.14	'Afternoon Talisman'
19.52	'North Briton'
22.45	'Tynesider'

*Without an official headboard